PERSPEC1
SWAGGER

Swagger *is a veritable encyclopedia of knowledge, information, advice, and wisdom that <u>every</u> person should read, preferably, while still a young adult.*

–Dr. Jerry Polson, Professor of Physics (theoretical nuclear), Department Chair, Graduate Dean, and Assistant Vice-President of Academic Affairs (Retired)

You have hit a home run here. Absolutely brilliant. Poetic. Touched my soul.

–Brent, Administrator, The Hill

Wow! Very good stuff.

–Abe, a media producer

This book has merit and is valuable for anyone who chooses to think.

–Victor, media executive, CEO, and musician

Fantastic!

–Lisa, a mom and teacher

I am adopted from China. The Chapter "Who Are You?" really touched me. I believe other people my age will be touched as well.

–Maggie, a Freshman in college

I immersed myself in this superb work. Expertly presented.

–Nicole, a leadership consultant

I really enjoyed reading your book. It's valuable and sparked a lot of discussion.

–Tyler, an associate attorney

Great! I laughed out loud in places. Very progressive.

–Megan, a graduate student

This is my kind of book. I love every paragraph. **Swagger** *is the most encouraging thing I've read in a long time.*

–Will, a Freshman in college

Wonderful. Get this manuscript published!

–Parker, an advance reader of **Swagger** and Sophomore in college

Beautiful. Moving. Thanks for writing this book.

–Ross, a pastor

Wow! You have done a great thing here.

–Blake, former US Marine, founder of a company, father, and grandfather

Very good advice.

–Drew, a minister to college-age students

Such a well-written, insightful, and moving book about life.

–Oakley, a Senior in college and new wife

As a university professor and administrator, I've engaged with students for 30+ years. Surprisingly few of them have a "toolbox" sufficient for navigating the social, emotional, and spiritual turbulence they'll face as university students and beyond. **Swagger** *is such a toolbox.*

Many sections of this book I found riveting, and all are well-written, concise, and provocative. I'm certain they'll challenge your thinking as they did mine. **Swagger** *invites then equips us to engage life's difficult questions, to wrestle in physical and spiritual arenas, and to walk boldly and confidently in our understanding.*

–Dr. John Samuel Russin, Vice Chancellor
Emeritus, Louisiana State University

SWAGGER

PRESTON GILLHAM

PUBLICATION™

PUBLICATION™

Published and printed in the United States of America
by Bonefish Publication

2020 Wilshire Boulevard, Fort Worth, TX 76110

For bulk purchase discounts, please contact
Bonefish Publication: info@bonefishpublication.com.

For further information about *Swagger*, other works by the author, his blog,
or to contact the author about speaking engagements, or his guidance work,
please visit: PrestonGillham.com

Library of Congress Control Number: 2020908108

ISBN 978-0-9845103-5-1

DEDICATION

Love and serve mankind. Be instruments of peace.
Walk with God. Be innocent as a dove. Be shrewd like a serpent.

Now, go into the world:

Ada, Caedon, Carson, Jackson, Liam, Maya, and Preston[2]

I believe in each of you and love you like my own,

"Nothing is more difficult than to think well."

—Thomas Traherne

SWAGGER

BY

PRESTON GILLHAM

TABLE OF CONTENTS

1. Who I Am (in Part) 15

2. Rules 17

3. Where Did God Go? 27

4. Books and Folks. 33

5. It's Relative 37

6. Dates 49

7. The Bible. 59

8. Reading the Bible 65

9. History 69

10. Cause and Effect 77

11. Generalities 83

12. Good 89

13. Apologetics 95

14. Distant or Engaged. 103

15. Jesus Christ. 113

16. Let's Assume 119

17. Why is Christianity Unique? 123

18. Can Christianity Be Proven? 125

19. What is a Christian? 129

20. Blame. 133

21. Shame. 143

22. Quitting. 155

23. Capital 165

24. Composure 171

25. Going Through Hell 175

26. Crouching Dragon. 181

27. Forgiving 189

28. Peace 199

29. Tears. 205

30. Swagger 209

31. Sex 213

32. Distinct Versus Separate. 217

33. Worth. 231

34. The Media 239

35. Old People and Ideas 243

36. Who Are You?. 249

37. My View of You 255

38. Who I Am 261

Appendix A 265

What Now? 269

Suggested Resources 273

Suggested Websites 277

Acknowledgements 279

Contact Information & Bulk Pricing 281

CHAPTER 1

WHO I AM (IN PART)

I am the descendant of immigrants, scoundrels, patriots, ministers, and courageous individuals. All that made them runs in my veins.

I discovered America in Wilson, Oklahoma during a snowstorm. I am the oldest of four, all brothers. Mason and Wade are dead. Will and I remain, two of four.

I'm a therapist who learned more about humanity studying history than he did studying human behavior. From grappling with the concerns of individuals, I moved into business and began grasping what it took to guide groups of people. I have traveled and worked all over North America, the Caribbean, Europe, western Asia, and parts of the Middle East.

These days, I spend most of my time writing, primarily fiction.

I'm married to Dianne, an absolutely lovely woman. We have twins, Alex and Anna. They both live in heaven.

I was born and raised in Oklahoma, studied in Missouri, and moved to Fort Worth, Texas in 1982. Texas is home, but the red dirt of Oklahoma formed my bones.

From the bottom of my heart, thank you for reading my book. I'm honored. To enter your world, speak into your soul, and offer thoughts is a respect you have granted and one that I treasure.

CHAPTER 2

RULES

For our annual fly fishing trip, my brothers and I selected the Provo River in Utah. By the time we rendezvoused in the Salt Lake City airport, our demanding work weeks had taken their toll. We retrieved our rental car, located our hotel, and dropped our bags.

We inquired at the front desk about dinner. The lady named an array of great options. We also asked about a place to play a game or two of pool, but it was as if the receptionist had never considered this question before. Thinking that a bar would have a pool table, we asked her to recommend a pub. You'd think we asked about a bus to the moon.

It only makes sense that Salt Lake would not have a bar on every corner, but no pubs at all? No place to play pool?

I don't recall how we discovered The Dead Goat Saloon, but it was the only option we could find. It was located in a basement and accessed through a dimly lit door. It felt weird, and dodgy, like a dead goat I guess—how does one of those feel? It certainly felt like a dark dive. We paused at the top of the steps considering the dingy entrance. One of us must have stepped because the other two followed.

A guy greeted us as we walked in, "May I help you?" This was odd. Pubs don't usually have greeters.

Nodding at the empty pool table to my left, I said, "Yes, we'd like to play a couple games of pool."

"Are you members?"

"Members of what?"

"Members of The Dead Goat Saloon?"

We looked around. This was not a country club, certainly not a typical Members Only establishment.

"No, we're not members," I said. "We're from out of town, going fishing tomorrow, and just want to play a game of pool."

"Well, you have to be a member," the guy said.

"How do you become a member?" Wade asked.

"You have to be sponsored."

"Sponsored? Into The Dead Goat Saloon?" Will's tone was indignant, but he said what all three of us were thinking.

"That's right. Sponsored."

There was silence as we digested this rule. After a moment, the greeter said, "I think the guy at the far end of the bar would be willing to sponsor you."

We squinted through the haze. A disheveled man, hunched over a longneck bottle, sat alone staring into space.

"The guy down there with the trucker hat?" I asked.

The greeter nodded.

"So how much is the membership fee?" Wade inquired.

The greeter said, "If you buy him a beer, that should cover it."

Seriously. And just like that, we were members. If you are ever in Salt Lake, let me know. Rules are rules, but I'm a member.

Some rules you have to abide by, like sponsorship into The Dead Goat Saloon, stopping at red lights, or like buying a fishing license. But sometimes rules need to be broken—and I'm going to break a few in the pages that follow.

Not simply to break rules, but to manage standards that prevent us from achieving our best. At times, I will slough off dictates that impede our pace or redefine an expectation when I believe it limits what's possible.

There is what I think of as the hook rule. It says that as a writer I must hook you—seize your attention and interest—within the first few seconds of your reading, or at the outside, at least midway through the first page. I grasp the rule, but I bristle at its limitations.

There's a study that says your attention span is less than a goldfish's.[1] The study is probably true for its subjects, but this can't be true for you or you would have stopped reading before now.

I understand you need a literary hook—a sharp-pointed statement that catches your attention. We all do. I will deliver and set those hooks, but my style is more robust than a rule designed to hook a goldfish.

I want you to read my writing, but I'm more dedicated to creating a literary experience for you that delivers a cogent message than I am about staying within the bounds of predictable writing style. I'm asking you to trust me even if I prove unorthodox about when I present the hook to you.

Then there is the pronoun rule, which recently changed. The revised rule says that I must mix the gender of my pronouns to demonstrate that I'm broadminded. I grasp the spirit of the revised rule, but its application is awkward when written. My job as a writer is to write sharp, clear lines that escort you to our literary destination. Awkward usage does not facilitate that intent for either of us.

---

1 Wyzowl. "The Human Attention Span." *Wyzowl.com.* <https://www.wyzowl.com/human-attention-span/>. Accessed 4 April 2020.

If I use "woman" or "she" or "her," I'm referring to a female. If I use "man" or "he" or "him," I could be referring to a particular male, or to mankind, which includes both males and females. Let the context of the page guide you.

In Christian circles, there is the proselyte rule, i.e. an evangelistic expectation. If I'm a Christian, or if I'm writing about Christian ideas, then it is my obligation to convert you to Christianity.

My objective in these pages is not to tell you what to believe. Rather, my *raison d'etre*—my reason for writing—is to inspire you to reason, to help you think clearly, about important subjects. I've not taken pen in hand to proselytize you.

About a third of my chapters relate directly to faith, the Bible, Christianity, or God. There are two reasons for this.

First, my university studies in the liberal arts, and my subsequent professional life, included these topics directly and indirectly. They remain relevant and are what I know best.

Second, these subjects are inescapable. One way or another, everyone must contend with them—or everyone should if they are going to be a responsible human being.

I once met a man who wrote for *The New York Times Magazine.* He was considered brilliant. Educated at Yale, highly acclaimed, articulate, and also an avowed atheist.

Being writers, he and I were talking about writing techniques. I asked if he wrote by hand or at a keyboard.

"By hand," he said, patting his shoulder bag. "I always carry a legal pad."

I named the most famous Christian author of the time, noting that he also wrote by hand. The man said, "I don't know who that is."

We talked some more. I casually mentioned another Christian author's writing style. Again he said, "I don't know who that is."

One more time, later in our conversation, I circled back and mentioned the writing style of the most noted Christian apologist of the day. "I don't know who that is."

All while listening, and smiling, and nodding, I thought, *You are an ardent atheist, yet you have not investigated matters of God's existence and your belief with enough thoroughness to recognize the most famous Christian authors and apologists of the day, let alone consider their writings. Your intellect is unenlightened, your belief without substance, your atheism a declaration of ignorance. Whatever you may be, you are not brilliant.*

Bob Dylan was hailed as the Shakespeare of my generation. In 2016 he was awarded the Nobel Prize for literature. In one piece he wrote, "Indeed you're gonna have to serve somebody / Well, it may be the devil or it may be the Lord / But you're gonna have to serve somebody."[2]

I've not written *Swagger* to convert you—proselytize you—to my beliefs. Rather, I've written in an attempt to look important matters square in the eye. It's tempting to procrastinate or rationalize about important subjects,

---

2 Dylan, Bob. "Gotta Serve Somebody." *Slow Train Coming.* Special Rider Music. New York, NY. 1979. *BobDylan.com.* <.http://www.bobdylan.com/songs/gotta-serve-somebody/>. Accessed, 4 April 2020.

especially if they feel risky, imposing, or threatening. But sooner or later, important issues come to the surface. Better to face them now, head-on, than suffer regret later.

Most books are created around a theme—each chapter crafted to segue into the next chapter, thus satisfying the rule of continuity.

Swagger is close, but not quite traditional in this regard. That is, the chapters don't connect like links in a chain. The theme of *Swagger* is critical thinking, not a particular subject, per se.

I didn't start thinking—thinking critically—until I was a Junior in college. It's not like I realized I needed to develop this skill, or even that I lacked it.

Rather, as you will read, I found myself drowning intellectually. My faith was capsized. My moorings had come loose and my confidence was adrift. I was confused. I had no idea how to manage my predicament, but I knew I needed to figure it out. It was sink or swim.

I regained my bearings, but discovered my twenties presented additional dilemmas. The same for my thirties. Ditto in my forties, fifties, and now my sixties. I used to think life was about solving problems. In one sense it is, since life is a plethora of problems, but at a more rudimentary level, life is fundamentally about being able to think, to reason, to comprehend, and then to adjust.

Like this book's structure, life doesn't have the continuity I expected when I was a younger man. But it has principles, and touchpoints, and axioms that

I return to again and again. The chapters in this short volume cover subjects that were scattered along my lifetime of living. By binding them together, I offer not a roadmap, but markers to help you navigate life, thought, and belief.

The beauty of breaking the continuity rule is that if you are reading a chapter that doesn't resonate with you, you can save it for later and move to the next chapter. Each chapter stands on its own. This said though, there is method to the madness of how I organized the Table of Contents.

Then, there is the footnote rule. I run slipshod over this one.

I'm aware that there are rules for endnotes, footnotes, and bibliographies. As you've already noticed, I've opted to use footnotes for *Swagger*. I've also opted to not include a bibliography. When you look at the notes, don't mistake my form as exemplary of the footnotes rule. I broke that rule and created my own form, a blend of notes and bibliography that better suited my purposes as I wrote with you in mind.

I tell you what I think in these chapters, but my motive for doing so is a sincere attempt to help you think, not tell you what to think, or give you answers to the questions. Think of it as my attempt to model ways that I think and reason about the variety of subjects in *Swagger*.

I trust your sensibility. Most people want their life to work. To use a fishing metaphor, why should I give you a fish when I can show you how to fish?

You are my reader. I am your author. At the turning of the final page, I hope we are friends. In my value system, friends don't give friends answers, per se.

Mostly, friends stand side-by-side come hell or high water. They trust each other.

"Open conversations build trust. Overcoming stress and challenging environments builds trust. Working through emergencies and seeing how people react builds trust."[3] These observations are made by two men who should know, Jocko Willink and Leif Babin, both Navy SEALs retired. In a variety of ways, this is my attempt in *Swagger*. Open conversations. Questions. Stress, demand, and confronting change. Thinking, reacting, settling, and acting. In reasoning together, trust will belong to us.

After a short night of playing pool at The Dead Goat Saloon, my brothers and I returned to the hotel. The night receptionist was now on duty. She looked up as we entered. "Wow. You guys are brothers." There was no denying that, either by appearance or blood. We smiled and waved as we trekked through the lobby.

We fished the Provo River the next day. It was tough. No fish bites, lots of bug bites.

I sat down and stared at the river. The current was fast, not many holding spots for fish, rocky, and a bit murky. None of the bugs were lighting on the water. They were all lighting on me, so no top-water feeding action. I thought about the fly I had on the end of my line. It was a good choice.

---

3 Willink, Jocko and Babin, Leif. *Extreme Ownership: How U.S. Navy SEALs Lead and Win*. St. Martin's Press. New York, NY. 2017. P. 191.

One of the rules in fishing—at least, it's one of my rules—is that if it's not obvious why the fish aren't biting, then fish deeper. I recalled this rule and added weight to my line so it would sink faster and deeper in the raucous current.

A very nice brown trout seized my fly on the next cast. Some rules you can break, but others it pays to obey.

Questions for Consideration

1. After reading the brief biographical sketch of Preston, do you like him and believe he will be honest with you? Do you have reservations about him, and if so, what are those?

2. With Preston's biographical chapter, and this chapter about rules, what are your expectations for what follows in Swagger?

3. Preston tells us up front that he is going to break a few rules. At what point in life is it okay to honor some rules and either disregard or reconstruct other rules?

CHAPTER 3

WHERE DID GOD GO?

I came of age in the 1960s and 1970s. I walked the stage of Durant (Oklahoma) High School in 1974 with 152 classmates. I registered for the draft (into the military), and planned to go to college.

Ninety-two years before I crossed the stage of Durant High School, Friedrich Nietzsche announced the death of God. However, the world was distracted by the implementation of socialism in Europe, so it wasn't until the 1960s that the world took note of God's passing and set about managing life without Him.

According to Nietzsche and his successors, God didn't exactly die. Rather, He was killed by us because He was no longer necessary. The Enlightenment Age established that man's ability to reason proved he was self-sufficient, a god, and that it was only a matter of time until mankind achieved a utopian society. The monarchy, the Church, and God were impediments and were to be thrown off.

Utopia. Perfection. These are grand ideals. The process by which utopia is achieved is humanism, i.e. the philosophical belief that humanity can recreate the Garden of Eden, achieve perfection, and establish utopia from within ourselves, without divine guidance, inspiration, or strength.

A magnificent belief in human ingenuity and utopian aspiration merits a look backward to see how things went.

Between 1882, the year God died, and 1982, humankind killed more of our fellows than in any other century. At the turn of the twentieth century, in order to launch our socialistic dream, we assassinated more political leaders than any other time before or since. From 1914 to 1918 we conducted the "war to end all wars," named such because it was so horrific. There was no winner. Everyone left standing simply quit and went home. For the next two decades, we languished in economic depression and runaway inflation. In the 1930s, our senses convulsed and we staged for a reprise of the war to end all wars—and carried it out. From 1933 to 1945 we slaughtered multiple millions of our fellow human beings and only concluded our killing of one another by the use of an atomic weapon. Whereupon we entered into an interminable Cold War, nuclear winter, mutually-assured destruction (MAD), and regional conflicts like the Korean War and the Vietnam Conflict.

One has to wonder if we were not better off when God was alive.

When our philosophers announced the death of God, my generation heaved and upheaved. Our music was angry, our hair long, our parents quiet, our brains drugged, and society frowned upon us as our friends died in the mud and the blood and the tears of Southeast Asia. When they came home from half-a-world-away, they were shamed by their country because of what they did for the politicians who required them to go. Someone dubbed us the Boomer Generation.

The Boomers built lives and had children who are the parents, grandparents, professors, business leaders, government officials, and mentors of Generation X, the Millennials, and Gen Z. As I write, the last of the Boomers are retiring.

Many Boomers decided God was not dead after all. In fact, the early 1970s produced one of the greatest spiritual revivals in American history. Still, the raucous, disillusioned soil of the late twentieth century rooted the people who built the world you are inheriting and bequeathed to you a culture with a marginalized God, a chip on its shoulder, and a wildly successful business resumé.

Culture is what it is, but it's something to be reconciled. If you want to understand a man, walk a mile in his shoes. Ideas, thoughts, experiences, and social influences have consequences.

The Bible says we look at life through a dim, foggy glass.[4] When it's foggy, you can't see very far ahead or behind. Thus, the purpose of this essay is to offer historical perspective that clears some of the fog you will encounter on your journey.

---

4 1 Corinthians 13:12. *Holy Bible. English Standard Version* (ESV). Crossway Bibles. Wheaton, IL. 2007.

As you consider thoughts and concepts, whether at your university, in the media, at work, or sitting around the table, remember who you are, what formed you, and where the people before you came from. We are all products of life's influences.

Seek first to understand, then to speak. This is the wise course of action.

By the way, Nietzsche was wrong.

But humanity had to test his idea for themselves—and some of those you encounter are still behaving as if God doesn't exist. History's record reveals Nietzsche's false declaration cost us dearly.

Don't fall for the lie, Nietzsche's or the Enlightenment. Humankind's track record without God's involvement is a train wreck.

God is not dead.

In fact, not only is He not dead, He doesn't even sleep. He's very much alive, active, and engaged. He is near you, the Bible says. And, He's interested in you.[5]

---

5 Cf. Psalm 121:4; Hebrews 4:12; Psalm 46:1; 145:18; Ephesians 2:13; James 4:8; John 10:10; 1:12. *Holy Bible. English Standard Version* (ESV). Also, *Holy Bible. New American Standard Version* (NASB). Lockman Foundation. La Habra, CA. 1975.

Questions for Consideration

1. What was it about the Enlightenment period that enticed men like Friedrich Nietzsche to believe God was dead and mankind able to achieve perfection and a utopian society?

2. Beyond what's mentioned in this chapter, what do you know about Baby Boomers?

3. What's your thought about the last paragraph of the chapter?

CHAPTER 4

BOOKS AND FOLKS

In five years, you will largely be the product of the books you read and the people you hang out with.

My cousin-in-law, who teaches high school physics, told me, "My students will not read. They just won't do it." Pew reported in 2019 that 27% of adults haven't read a book this year.[6] They report the readership mean is 4 books per year. The Bureau of Labor and Statistics found that Americans over the age of 15 spend only 16.8 minutes each day reading for pleasure.[7]

My first sentence stands.

6 Perrin, Andrew. "Who Doesn't Read Books in America?" *Factank News in the Numbers*. September 26, 2019. Pew Research Center. <https://www.pewresearch.org/fact-tank/2019/09/26/who-doesnt-read-books-in-america/>. Accessed, 21 April 2020.

7 Hess, Abigail. "24 Percent of American Adults Haven't Read a Book in the Past Year—Here's Why." *CNBC.com*. January 29, 2019. <https://www.cnbc.com/2019/01/29/24-percent-of-american-adults-havent-read-a-book-in-the-past-year--heres-why-.html>. Accessed, 21 April 2020.

If you don't read, it is imperative that you begin. Turn pages, swipe, or listen to an audio book. Your options are wide open. But you simply must read—and for longer than 17 minutes.

As I write, the world ebbs and flows and "communicates" in Twitter bursts that average only 33 characters.[8] Relationships are formed by visual imagery on Instagram, Snapchat, TikTok, etc.

Two things you need to know: 1) By the time you read this, the mediums mentioned will have changed. 2) It is impossible for you to construct informed thinking by reliance upon photographs and a max of 280 characters on a tiny screen.

Is this the opinion of an older generation that doesn't understand or appreciate a younger generation? If we were talking music, maybe. If we were talking style, probably. If we were talking hair, certainly.

But, we're not.

We are talking reading, exposing yourself to big ideas, other worlds, different and new concepts developed over the course of sequential words, paragraphs hinging on the one before and the one following, for 180 pages, all bound into a volume. You need this cohesion to think and you get it one place, and one place only: good books (note: there are also crummy books).

---

8 Perez, Sarah. "Twitter's Doubling of Character Count from 140 to 280 had Little Impact on Length of Tweets." *TechCrunch.com*. October 30, 2018. <https://techcrunch.com/2018/10/30/twitters-doubling-of-character-count-from-140-to-280-had-little-impact-on-length-of-tweets/>. Accessed, 21 April 2020.

Mark Twain is attributed as saying, "The man who does not read has no advantage over the man who cannot read."[9] In other words, don't consider yourself literate if you do not read on a regular basis.

General "Mad Dog" James Mattis estimates he has a library of seven thousand volumes. Reading his book, it appears he remembers what's in each of them. Incredible. Typical of his style, General Mattis writes, "If you haven't read hundreds of books, learning from others who went before you, you are functionally illiterate."[10]

Argue if you wish, but for all the flux between generations—hair, music, sexual mores, style—one thing is true of the human species, and it has been true since mankind first appeared: We are a relational, communicative, pack animal. We learn by imitation, exchanged words, physical engagement, and the transfer of culture and thought through mutually respectful relationships.

All of this you will gain through two things: reading and hanging out. In five years, you will be the product of the books you read and the people you spend time with.[11]

---

9 Sylvester, Brad. "Fact Check: Did Mark Twain say, 'The man who does not read has no advantage over the man who cannot read?'" *CheckYourFact.com*. September 12, 2019. <https://checkyourfact.com/2019/09/12/fact-check-mark-twain-man-read-advantage-literacy/>. Accessed, 21 April 2020.

10 Mattis, James N. *Call Sign Chaos: Learning to Lead*. Random House. New York, NY. 2019. P. 237.

11 I have included a reading list at the back of this book. It includes some of my favorite books as well as a few of the books I've referenced in *Swagger*.

Questions for Consideration

1. What have you read lately? When do you read? What gets in your way of reading?

2. Think about the 3-5 people with whom you spend the most time. Are you satisfied with their influence in your life? Your influence in their lives? Any adjustments you'd like to make? If so, do you know how to make those adjustments and where to go if you could use assistance?

3. Some readers read in cycles: e.g. a biography, a history, a novel, and repeat. Many people read daily for a duration. What might a workable reading schedule look like for you? What adjustments would you need to make for such a schedule to work?

CHAPTER 5

IT'S RELATIVE

John Mack Faragher wrote a fantastic biography of Daniel Boone, the legendary Kentucky woodsman. Mr. Faragher recounts that Boone was once asked if he'd ever been lost. Daniel said, "I can't say as ever I was lost, but I was bewildered once for three days."[12]

Years ago, I went to Colorado with some buddies. They were hunting elk, I was tagging along. They put me in charge of navigation, which back in the day was done with a map and compass, not a GPS.

A compass works off of Earth's North Magnetic Pole, located around Hudson Bay, not the true North Pole—where Santa lives—located at the top of the globe. The imaginary line between true north and magnetic north creates

12 Faragher, John Mack. *Daniel Boone: The Life and Legend of an American Pioneer.* Henry Holt and Company. New York, NY. 1992. Page 64.

the zero-degree line on a map. This line is not vertical, but is tilted slightly northwest to southeast.

If you are east or west of the zero-degree line, you have to adjust your compass or your navigation will be off by increasing numbers of degrees the farther east or west you go from the zero line. This adjustment is called magnetic declination, or just declination. When using a map and compass, you must figure out the declination of your location and adjust your compass bearings or you will miss your target, i.e. get lost.

So, the declination in Nashville is zero since it is located on the zero-degree line. Where I live in Texas, the declination is eight degrees. In Colorado, the declination requires twelve degrees of compass adjustment.

To put this in perspective, if you fail to adjust for declination in Colorado, after you walk a mile you will be about 880 feet left of where you intend to go. If you are aiming for a town that's a quarter-mile away, you'll be okay. But if you are hiking five miles and aiming for your truck, you will miss the truck by about 4,400 feet.

And, that's what happened to us.

"Where are we?" Mel said.

I wanted so badly to say the map was wrong. But, I confessed, "I forgot to allow for declination." Not only did I not have a reliable course to the truck, I didn't even have a known location on the map—and it was pitch dark.

It would have been silly if I had said, "Oh well, I didn't like this map anyway. We are where we are—relative to us. We'll just start from here and call it good. Follow me, guys."

Our fate in the mountains was absolutely tied to the map, the location of our truck, and where we were. The problem I had created though was that I had no idea where we were in relation to the map or the truck. Any chance of finding our ride to the cabin was marginalized. We were lost, and as dark and cold set in, we were in trouble.

Ultimately, we located our truck, but not before some bewildered wandering in the woods.

Now, let's take the analogy out of the woods and apply it to life. Life is not measured in feet or degrees. Life is measured in years and navigated by ideas tied to standards, not unlike the directional marks on a map. Start off wrong, or use a flawed life-map, or mismanage life's standards and there's no telling where you are going to wind up.

Our hike back to the truck that night got serious right quick. We were lost because I failed to respect two navigational standards: my map and magnetic declination.

Similarly, even though losing our bearings as a people creates peril, expansive swaths of society either dismiss or do not recognize standard truths, choosing instead to navigate life by relative truth, i.e. whatever they call true and adopt is what they declare truth to be.

This raises the question: Can you know anything with certainty and does it matter?

In some cases, yes. There are truths called laws. If you jump off the garage, you will fall. Newton named this the Law of Gravity. In philosophy, there is the law of noncontradiction: If something is true, its opposite must be false.

Okay, so there are laws that are true. But does truth exist?

It's an old question. Pontius Pilate, the Roman governor of Judea from 26-37 CE, asked Jesus during His trial, "What is truth?"[13] He assumed there wasn't any such thing since his question was rhetorical. How to sentence Jesus for his alleged crime was therefore relative to what Pontius Pilate felt was right.

By definition, "truth" is narrow and self-limiting. If something is true, then whatever is outside of that is false. You'll notice that we are bumping up against the law of noncontradiction mentioned earlier.

Think about my situation in the mountains: There was a true path back to our truck, not a relative path that I could declare as true just because I didn't want to acknowledge I was lost. In truth, I either figured out where we were in relation to the map or we stayed lost.

Therefore, the notion of relative truth doesn't work. Truth is what it is and it will always be this in every situation or it isn't true. Relative means conditional, relative to circumstance, to me, to whim, to culture, to whatever.

Something cannot be true and relative as well.

---

13 John 18:38. NASB.

But take note: Even though the term is senseless, "relative truth" (or relativism) prevails.

At heart, we humans have ideas about what we want and we will push, and shove, and grasp to have what we want. As the saying goes, we want to have our cake and eat it too.

Relativism asks, if I want to have my cake and eat it too, why shouldn't I? Who's to say that this boundary, this standard, this truth, applies to me? Figure out what's right for you and leave me alone. Why can't we all just get along and be more understanding—be more tolerant?

Tolerance sounds reasonable, civilized, and polite. But ideas have consequences. If truth exists, then relative truth is a rationalization to either avoid or deny what is true.

Let's take four cases-in-point and examine relativism: sexual mores, constitutional government, biblical legitimacy, and civil society.

It used to be that western society accepted truth as located in the Bible. For example, the seventh commandment says, "You shall not commit adultery."[14] Of course, people have been committing adultery since sex was invented, but once upon a time we accepted that doing so was wrong based upon the truth of the seventh commandment.

Today, adultery may or may not be wrong. Let me illustrate based upon what I was taught in grad school and expected to model in my practicums to become a therapist.

---

14 Exodus 20:14. NASB.

My client, Joe, tells me—his therapist—that he's having an affair with Sally. Who am I to question Joe? I'm neither the clarion voice of sexual truth nor the arbiter of Joe's sex life. What is right is relative to what Joe and Sally want. After all, they're consenting adults. Therefore, my charge as a therapist is to assist Joe in determining what's best relative to him.

What then, of Lucy, Joe's offended wife?

Well, Lucy will come to therapy and figure out what's right for her given Joe's affair with Sally. Perhaps she loses 25 pounds, has her teeth whitened, and moves in with Frank. We are all sexual creatures, Frank understands her, and she's comforted. She's found her truth and it's right for her. In the therapy world, this outcome is a success.

What of Frank's kids who are asking why he's sleeping with Lucy and not their mommy, Jane?

Meanwhile, Jane has hired the meanest of divorce lawyers and is plotting to get even with Frank while angling for full custody of their children. She also has breast augmentation and a nose job. It's the right thing for her to do given the situation.

In this instance, who has sex with who is relative—a personal judgment call. The only rule is whether you have "safe" sex or not. Everything else is relative, including each individual responding as seems right to them.

Is this true? Relatively true? Absolutely true?

Joe has one answer, Sally another, Lucy another, Frank a fourth view, and Jane another yet. The kids? They're resilient and will be okay, or so the rationale goes. We don't tolerate asking how relative truth is working out for everyone, and heaven forbid we tell Joe he must get out of bed with Sally based upon the seventh commandment. That's intolerant, narrow, and unenlightened.

If there is no standard, then everyone is free to do what seems best to them, as relative to them. Everyone else must accept and manage the consequences of relative behavior or be deemed intolerant.

But the implications of relative navigation through life becomes bewildering pretty quickly.

Let's get out of bed and into government and look at another example: There is debate in American society over the United States Constitution. Some say it is a static document that should be interpreted in its original language and intent. Others say it is a living document and should be interpreted in spirit, not in word, to make it more relevant. After all, how could the framers of the Constitution anticipate in 1776 the issues facing us in the twenty-first century? We should adjust the Constitution to reflect society, not vice versa.

As I write this chapter, society is convulsing over what the Constitution means by the First and Second Amendments as well as Article II, Section 1 regarding the Electoral College. One side argues one truth while the opposite side argues another truth.

If the Constitution is relative, then who decides what is true for us today?

You say, "The Supreme Court decides." Except the Court's justices are split on the question of how to view the Constitution: static or relative? For one side, the founding document is a fixed point from which to navigate. For the other side, the founding document was a good idea in 1776 but carries only relative force in today's debate.

If the latter perspective is applied, and the document is relatively true, then everything dependent upon the Constitution is open to question: e.g. constitutional law, the courts, Congress, national election laws, bearing of firearms, freedom of speech, any Federal agency that establishes standards—the FAA, CIA, FBI, IRS—as well as the inalienable rights you enjoy to life, liberty, and the pursuit of happiness, not to mention your freedom to congregate, to religious freedom, to freedom of speech....

If there is no agreed upon, recognized standard, then we must continuously negotiate new norms and standards. This seems reasonable at first blush—even tolerant, open-minded, progressive—but return to my experience in the Colorado mountains: If I said to Mel and Charlie, "Never mind the map. I've got good instincts. My gut's saying we should head that direction," they might think themselves progressive to hike along with me, but as they walk their fate is tied to my gut and the only real truth is folded up in my pocket.

I mentioned the Bible earlier. It used to be that the Bible was viewed as factually true. Many conservative churches still believe this and have in their statements of belief that they hold the Bible to be infallible and inspired, suitable to guide life and liberty.

Generally speaking, in the nineteenth century, a movement arose that evaluated the Bible scientifically. First to be thrown out were the miracles. Every scientist knows humans can't walk on water. Next was a parsing of what Jesus *meant* to say as opposed to what He *said*.

Eventually, the original text unraveled like a cheap rug and there was a complete rewrite of the Bible reflective of science and our judgment relative to modern thinking. So, rather than an authoritative, true document that guides life and society, the Bible became a relatively true, supporting document where deemed applicable.

What objective sense does it make to assess the Bible's veracity with scientific methodology because this seems right to you when the Bible is a metaphysical text not a science journal? Clearly, with such an approach, you don't have a prayer—pun intended—of accurately comprehending the biblical message. Yet, the textual critics proceeded, edited, and rewrote the Bible as suited them, based upon standards they held dear, but that the original authors knew nothing about.[15]

Relativism prevails and a book deemed authoritative—even divine—was declared untrue. To say otherwise is ignorant.

Here's an example from civil society where relative truth is clashing with empirical truth: In 1973, the Supreme Court heard the case of Roe versus Wade. They ruled in favor of Roe and abortion was legalized. Earlier standards believed the womb sacrosanct, but with Roe's passage, pregnancy became relative to a woman's decision about what she wished to do with her body.

---

15 These three paragraphs are high-level summary statements, generalizations to make a point, i.e. that the inspiration and veracity of the Bible came under scientific and textual critique that rendered a view of the Bible as suspect. This view conflicts with the view held by conservative theologians. Liberal Christianity amalgamated with Neo Orthodox theology to render varying perspectives about the Bible across the denominational landscape today. Consequently, there are denominations, e.g. Episcopal, Methodist, et al, that generally view biblical teaching as relative while there are other denominations and churches, e.g. Bible Churches, most Baptist, some Presbyterian, that view the Bible as divinely inspired and thus relevant to authoritatively guide life and practice.

A half-century and over 52 million abortions later,[16] Roe v. Wade is being challenged in the Supreme Court. Pro-choice advocates and the media blame conservatives for the legal tests of abortion, but that's simplistic. What's actually transpiring is that the relative truth from 1973 is crumbling under the weight of scientific, empirical truth fifty years later.

Medical science has advanced exponentially since Roe was passed. Abortion as a relative argument based upon how a particular woman governs her body is now contrasted against medical science being able to hear an infant heartbeat at 6 weeks gestation and demonstrate fetal viability as early as 22-24 weeks gestation.[17] Research is emerging that the "mass of tissue" feels early embryonic pain and reacts.[18]

Abortion proponents are scrambling to justify the procedure. Denying that a fetus is an embryonic human being is no longer tenable.

In other words, as medical insight comes to light, women (and men) are presented with a different decision when facing an unwanted pregnancy: Rather than, it is my [relative] right to have an abortion and govern my body as I wish, the question is, can I commit infanticide (i.e. kill my own child) rather than accept responsibility for this human life maturing in my womb?

---

16 Noble, Jason. "Fact Check: 50 Million Abortions Claim Checks Out." *The Des Moines Register.* March 17, 2015. <https://www.desmoinesregister.com/story/news/politics/reality-check/2015/03/06/million-abortions-claim-checks/24530159/>. Accessed, 21 April 2020.

17 Danielsson, Krissi. "Premature Birth and Survival Statistics." *VeryWellFamily.com.* April 20, 2020. < https://www.verywellfamily.com/premature-birth-and-viability-2371529>. Accessed, 17 July 2020.

18 Charlotte Lozier Institute. "Fact Sheet: Science of Fetal Pain." February 19, 2020. <https://lozierinstitute.org/fact-sheet-science-of-fetal-pain/>. Accessed, 4 July 2020.

Lewis writes, "For the wise men of old the cardinal problem had been how to conform the soul to reality, and the solution had been knowledge, self-discipline, and virtue." He goes on to observe that the problem today is how to subdue reality to the wishes of mankind.[19]

From being lost in Colorado, to whether adultery is appropriate or not, the Constitution static or relative, the Bible inspired or flawed, and how civil society updates its view of abortion, these illustrations from physical, national, spiritual, and civic life are designed to unmask relativism so you can assess how you determine to proceed.

Does life have coordinates and truths, or can life be lived relative to your wishes, preferences, and expediency?

Who's to say what's right and what's wrong—about the Bible, abortion, history, the Constitution, who you sleep with, or anything else?

I discovered studying history that the premise of the biblical book of Ecclesiastes is correct: there's nothing new under the sun.[20] The tension between truth and relativism was just as fraught in Pontius Pilate's thinking as it is in today's thinking. But whereas Pontius Pilate recognized relativism and declared it, modern society has adopted it as the barometer of truth.

---

19 Lewis, C.S. *The Abolition of Man*. Harper One, a division of Harper Collins. New York, NY. 1944, 1974. P. 77.

20 Ecclesiastes 1:9. NASB.

I've written this chapter to shed light on the dilemma between truth and relativism. You don't know what you don't know. But as an enlightened person, you can seek truth instead of progressing through life relatively with your eyes wide-shut.

Theoretically, being an adult means you think clearly, assess carefully, and draw reasoned conclusions with your eyes wide-open. If you can do this relatively, so be it, but it's a tricky business. If not, then a quest to locate a resolute standard is the wise course of action.

In the end, that's how Mel, Charlie, and I located our truck, avoided a bivouac under a fir tree, and slept comfortably in our cabins.

Questions for Consideration

1. Does life have coordinates and truths, or can life be lived relative to your wishes, preferences, and expediency?

2. How do you think society's standards should be established?

3. Sex, government, abortion rights or standards, and the Bible: The chapter explored the viability of each to guide your life from an authoritative or reasoned position. What are your thoughts?

Chapter 6

DATES

When I say we need to talk about dates, I don't mean fun times with your significant other. I mean those ancient times and epochs you hear stated as unimpeachable fact.

Here's the deal: The farther back in time you gaze, the less reliable dates become. Beyond a few thousand years, you require something else to make a judgment about time.

For example: Determining what happened during the Civil War (1861-1867) can be pretty reliable. People wrote letters and kept journals. Armies and businesses retained secretaries. Governments had clerks who kept meeting minutes. Many of these documents are dated. Thus, what Joe was doing on Thursday the 12th can be known—maybe.

Even in the late nineteenth century there were plenty of people, especially the disadvantaged, who had no idea when they were born, when they got married, or how to sign their names.

Once upon a time there was no standardized calendar. Some societies kept time based upon the moon, others the sun, still others the seasons.

As with many things a few hundred years ago, the church—the Catholic Church—was the driving force behind a standardized calendar. Their rationale? They needed to determine the date of Easter.

So, in 1582, in an effort to rectify the 11-minute failing of the Julian Calendar, Pope Gregory XIII established the Gregorian Calendar. While it's the calendar your life runs on today, it was still up for debate well into the eighteenth century.[21]

Think for a moment about the Christmas story. Luke's version begins, "Now it came about in those days that a decree went out from Caesar Augustus, that a census be taken of all the inhabited earth. This was the first census taken while Quirinius was governor of Syria."[22]

"In those days" indicates that the Apostle Luke probably doesn't know what the exact date is. But before you dismiss the man as ignorant and his book written by a hack, recall that he was a medical doctor and the literary

---

21 Hocken, Vigdis. "The Gregorian Calendar." *TimeandDate.com*. https://www.timeanddate.com/calendar/gregorian-calendar.html>. Accessed, 14 June 2020.

22 Luke 2:1-2. NASB.

structure of his book is composed in sophisticated grammar. While odd to our modern minds, it was not only good enough in Luke's mind to identify the time period as he did, it is quite remarkable that he went to the trouble he did to help us frame the birth of Christ during Quirinius' first census.

Many scholars believe Jesus was born in 4 BCE (also BC). Some say between 3-2 BCE. A few others, 6 BCE. The death of Herod seems a good benchmark, except there is historical doubt about when he died. You get the picture, I trust. As to Christmas being on December 25th, there's even more speculation.[23, 24]

Look back farther, beyond the Romans, beyond the Greeks, and exact dates are even harder to determine. Periods of time can usually be agreed upon to around 10,000 BCE, but only by piecing together bits of information from multiple sources.

Go farther back in history, past even the early texts of antiquity and the Bible, and reliable dates are stated by centuries of time. Farther back yet, to the origins of civilization, thought to be in the Tigris-Euphrates Rivers region, and honest times are stated in epochs of thousands of years.

So, what's the point?

---

23 Lucey, Candice. "When Was Jesus Born?" *Christianity.com*. <https://www.christianity.com/wiki/jesus-christ/when-was-jesus-born.html>. Accessed, 5 May 2020.

24 Sauter, Megan. "When Was Jesus Born–BC or AD?" *BiblicalArchaeology.org*. December 17, 2019. https://www.biblicalarchaeology.org/daily/people-cultures-in-the-bible/jesus-historical-jesus/when-was-jesus-born-bc-or-ad/>. Accessed, 5 May 2020.

Dates are proof. Dates are authoritative. Stating a date makes it sound like you know—for certain—and then based upon a date, this and that happened, and these other things couldn't have happened.

There are known dates because they're written down or because you can triangulate from various sources. Then there are period dates that are known, like in the Christmas story cited above, or like the dates for the Enlightenment Age or the Neolithic Age or the period of the Judges in the Bible.

There's not much debate about the period of time's designated name, but attributing events to these ancient times is the trick.

Proof of dates on ancient items is often based upon carbon dating. It can be fairly reliable—and it can be quite unreliable. There are lots of variables, especially the older an item is, where it is, and what it is. Rather than adopting a fact based upon carbon dating, my counsel is to note the date and see if it is complimented by other data. If so, fine. If not, that's fine as well. Keep thinking, exploring, and wondering with a broad and open mind. Beware of an ancient, declarative date.

Some things can be known and dated. Many ancient things cannot be dated, but that doesn't mean they aren't viable, legitimate, and knowable to some extent.

There's currently no way to know when the universe began. There's no way to date evolution. There's no way to know whether the creation account in Genesis is seven literal days or seven epochs of time. There's no way to know if one rules out the other. Beware of those who speak confidently in over-statements.

When it comes to the age of the universe, one measure used is the Hubble Constant. In September 2019 news broke that the age of the universe is not 13.7 billion years as everyone thought. Rather, it's 11.4 billion years old, 2.3 billion years younger than previously accepted.[25] But, hey! What's 2,300,000,000 years among friends? Right?

With this celestial age adjustment, Harvard astronomer Avi Loeb was interviewed for his opinion. Responding in an email, Dr. Loeb replied, "It is difficult to be certain of your conclusions if you use a ruler that you don't fully understand."[26]

Ten months after the 2.3 billion-year adjustment, an international team of astrophysicists confirmed—once and for all—that the universe is 13.8 billion years old, i.e. a million years older than first asserted. They made their determination by studying a photograph of the oldest light in the universe, what's known as the cosmic microwave, or the afterglow from the Big Bang. It's light occurring 380,000 years after the universe's birth.[27]

Astrophysicist Neelima Sehgal said, "We are restoring the 'baby photo' of the universe to its original condition, eliminating the wear and tear of time and space that distorted the image. Only by seeing this sharper baby photo

25 Borenstein, Seth. "Study Finds the Universe Might Be 2 Billion Years Younger." *Phys.org*. September 12, 2019. <https://phys.org/news/2019-09-universe-billion-years-younger.html>. Accessed, 21 April 2020.

26 Ibid.

27 Rice, Doyle. "Universe is `13.8 Billion Years Old, Scientists Confirm." *USAToday.com*. July 15, 2020. <https://www.usatoday.com/story/news/nation/2020/07/15/age-universe-13-8-billion-years-scientists-confirm/3287409001/>. Accessed, 17 July 2020.

or image of the universe, can we more fully understand how our universe was born."[28] Simone Aiola, the first to publish these findings, pronounced in a statement at Princeton, "…these difficult measurements are reliable."[29]

Yes, well.

There is also this to consider: "All the stars, planets and galaxies that can be seen today make up just 4 percent of the universe. The other 96 percent is stuff astronomers can't see, detect or even comprehend," Clara Moskowitz writes in Space.com.[30] Richard Panek, who wrote a book on this subject known as dark energy, said while speaking at CUNY, "The overwhelming majority of the universe is: who knows? It's unknown for now, and possibly forever."[31]

Not to be critical of the astronomical sciences, but definitive or declarative assertions regarding the age of the universe, how it began, what it is, how it works, and what it means can be a bit overstated it seems to me. I grasp the enthusiasm of those studying our universe, but personally I would be more comfortable if there was a hint of humility about what they know and don't know. If a medical doctor told me the procedure he was recommending had a 4 percent chance of success but that he was confident in recommending the procedure, I would run like the wind to find another doctor.

---

28 Ibid.

29 Ibid.

30 Moskowitz, Clara. "What's 96 Percent of the Universe Made Of? Astronomers Don't Know." *Space. com*. May 12, 2011. <https://www.space.com/11642-dark-matter-dark-energy-4-percent-universe-panek.html>. Accessed, 17 July 2020.

31 Ibid.

I met my friend Chuck for lunch. He's an optical physicist who grew up Jewish and wavers between agnosticism and atheism. I first heard about the 96 percent mystery of the universe from him. In between bites, I said, "Chuck, is it possible perhaps that somewhere in that 96 percent of the universe that is unknown and incomprehensible there might be room for God to exist?"

Chuck's reply was very much out of character for my normally gracious and genteel friend. "I see that differently!"

End of conversation.

I have now, and had then, so many questions for my buddy. What does he see differently? His reply didn't make sense then or now.

Chuck is a smart man. Given his religious quandaries, I wonder if he fears the implications of discovering he was mistaken about God, thus necessitating a will-to-will contention with who gets to run the universe, Chuck or God? I don't know. I'm speculating about my friend. Something about his declarative, definitive, categorical dismissal strikes me as having nothing to do with physics, astronomy, light, dark energy, or the universe.

Thinking about time and evolutionary theory, here are two thoughts: First, that evolution is accepted as true is a given, but that doesn't make it true. Scientific method is clear on how scientific theories are established and become laws. Evolutionary theory fails on multiple fronts to meet scientific rigor. Besides this, the times quoted with evolutionary theory are wild guesses. Until this becomes accurately quantifiable and the evolutionary process replicable, evolution should rise in our thoughts no higher than theory.

Second, everything had to get here some way. If the opening supposition is that God doesn't exist, or isn't involved, and evolution is our best guess, then the thinking goes that perhaps with enough eons of time to allow for myriad upon myriad of mutations and evolutions, creation can be postulated.

It's an intriguing idea. It sounds smart and it gives us all a multi-faceted path to run along, complete with nearly infinite studies to do, in such far-flung places as the Galápagos and Mars.

But, before you hitch your conclusions and convictions to evolution, consider carefully the time spans and what can and can't be known about dating.

There's an idiom—a manner of speaking—that you don't hear much these days, but years ago when people were confirming an appointment, they would say, "It's a date then." That phrase finalized their agreement.

In a phrase, that's my point in this chapter. Dates are definitive, authoritative, legitimizing, and affirming. If a date's attached, it really happened just that way, then and there.

This is all well and good, provided the date cited is truly known. Many aren't even though they sound like they are or are stated as such. Take note is my advice.

How dates are cited and constructed can be telltale signs about the veracity of a presentation.

I was listening to an interview with a microbiologist some months ago. He was an energetic and engaging speaker, and the topic was fascinating, but he persisted in legitimizing the various hypotheses put forward in his new book by citing "…the millions and millions of years of evolutionary development." The fourth or fifth time the scientist referenced the long history of evolutionary development, I began to wonder what he was telling his listeners about his new book.

Then, about two-thirds of the way through the interview, he paused and said to the host, "Can we just agree that evolution is true? I mean. Everyone believes it and speaks of it as true. Let's just declare it so and move on to other scientific pursuits." The interviewer agreed and the interview proceeded.

The citation of eons of years as documentation had my attention. The more the speaker spoke, and built his case upon millennia of years, the more pronounced my intellectual caution became. And then it came out: He needed his version of microbial evolutionary theory to be factual for his book to be legitimate, worth buying.

The dates helped me think. More accurately, understanding what dates do and can't do gave me insight into motive. While this is true, it's not every day a speaker shows you his hand like this one did. One of the primary reasons I'm writing this chapter is that it was many years from my initial dustup with dates before I comprehended how to consider times and epochs. By then, I had a fair bit of intellectual cleanup to do.

So, be astute about dates.

And come to think of it, even though I said this chapter wasn't about dating your significant other, being astute about who you are dating is also a smart move.

Questions for Consideration

1. Why does the subject of this chapter matter to your life?

2. Toward the end of the chapter, Preston told you about the interview he listened to with the microbiologist. He declared that we should all just agree to call evolution true since everyone speaks of it as true. What do you think?

3. There are those who believe the Bible is literally true. Perhaps you are one. How does the perspective put forward in this chapter regarding not knowing whether the creation record of Genesis is literally seven days, or seven periods, or seven of something else affect your belief in the Bible's literalness? What's necessary to reconcile any insecurity this creates for you?

CHAPTER 7

THE BIBLE

"Oh, my gosh! Steinbeck's *East of Eden* has to be the worst book ever. And they consider it a classic."

"Have you read George Orwell's *Animal Farm*? There are more contradictions than you can count. It's a total rant—about pigs."

"Yeah, or Shakespeare's *Macbeth*? 'Come out, damned spot.' The plot's so elementary. And the language! People don't talk like that."

"Well, I read J.R.R. Tolkien. Totally dumb! Talking trees, flying dinosaurs."

"In *Harry Potter* there are wizards. Crazy, but it made J.K. Rowling richer than the Queen."

"And the Bible. Talk about contradictions and stupid stuff! A burning bush that doesn't burn up? A talking snake? Walking on water."

If you are paying attention, you are a bit indignant at this literary rant. It's uncultured, shallow, and obtuse. Only a simpleton would discredit some of the greatest literary masterpieces of history.

But when you got to the criticism of the Bible, there was probably a touch of acceptance, agreement—something quiet in your head justifying the castigation. "Yeah, the talking snake always bothered me."

The most widely printed and read book in history is inferior literature.

Years ago, my atheist neighbor invited me to join a wine tasting group. The membership was composed primarily of men with whom he had taught, all smart guys. There were a couple of Harvard men, a Yale fellow, Princeton, Northwestern, and yours truly.

One of the guys—there were nine of us—was a history scholar. Over the course of fifteen years with these guys, every subject you can imagine came up, and more world events than can be numbered. Bill always knew the background—off the top of his head. It was like drinking wine with a living database.

About twice per year, for no apparent reason—you know how conversation ebbs and rambles—Bill would launch into a vitriolic harangue of what a stupid book the Bible is. Contradictions, dumb story lines, a universal flood, bad poetry... and inevitably conclude, "How can anyone read it and keep a straight face?"

Thankfully—or perhaps sadly—I'd heard it all before. It's accepted academic bias to make such comments about the Bible, as though the viewpoint is a given fact. So, when Bill would launch into his diatribe, soliciting nods from the other atheists and agnostics at the table, I would listen and let him run his mouth.

This happened each year, for probably a decade, until the night came when Bill started in. Two-thirds through his customary rant, Bill stopped and looked at me. It was the first time he'd looked me in the eye while disparaging a book he knew I'd devoted my life to studying. He smiled sheepishly and said, "I guess if I'm going to say these things, I should first read the book."

I nodded. "That might be a good idea, Bill. I'll help you get started if you like."

When Bill would start his rant, I always wondered what he was thinking. This was a smart man, extremely well read, a true scholar. How could he be so biased, not just because I didn't share his opinion, but because his outbursts were so blatantly unscholarly, uninformed, and as he admitted in the end, so profoundly biased and based upon absolutely zero actual information?

One of the rules of life is that when people overstate, they are usually trying to hide something. We all know that we should let the truth speak for itself. Embellishing it is not helpful.

The obvious question Bill needed to answer for himself is what motivated him to say such ridiculous things, regarding a subject he knew so little about, and a book he'd never read. His denunciations were all smoke, but where there's smoke, there's usually fire—an ember of something burning in Bill's soul that he either didn't want to acknowledge or was afraid to examine.

If the Bible is so easily dismissed, if it is indeed such a crummy piece of literature, or if its structure is so porous as to not hold intellectual water, then how is it that it is the most scrutinized book in history and remains the world's number one seller? How is it that the most examined book in history is the most resilient book in history? If it is so obviously flawed, as Bill ranted and railed, then how come so many scholars devote their lives to its study?

Here's something to keep in mind: Late in the nineteenth century a literary-scholarly movement arose in Germany that came to be called, German higher criticism. This helped birth over time what we think of as the modern historical method for literary criticism, i.e. the methodology you use for critical thinking about literature. Together, these approaches to historical literature created a new way to look at the Bible (and other ancient texts).

It would be unfair to say these scholars failed us. However, it would also be unfair to not point out a bias inherent in their approach.

In their zeal to analyze the Bible and antiquity, the critical approach they developed and that is in use today evaluates the texts in question by modern standards, i.e. mid-nineteenth century forward. This isn't all wrong, and it is insightful, but you should be aware as you read their opinions that they are often holding an ancient writer to a modern standard and critiquing that author for failing to document, cite sources, speaking in idioms, writing culturally, etc. That's not fair.

It's an arrogant approach to history and you will find it applied most frequently when considering a biblical text, although it is common in many aspects of historical thought. My observation is that many of the questions and critiques of the Bible, like those voiced by Bill, have their origin in the evaluations of scholars utilizing higher criticism.

To state the obvious: Of course the Bible—and any other older artifact of history—fails when held to a standard unknown to the original authors.

A second rule of life pertains to historical legitimacy: If something is old, established, and accepted by a scholarly community, it is worthy of historical trustworthiness.

Think of it this way: You might have something important to say from reading Homer's *Odyssey*. But put your opinion in a history paper at the university, and if your prof is worth his salt, your opinion will be ruled out as impertinent. Who are you to know anything about Homer? You haven't been alive long enough or read enough. Cite from Zenodotus, compare literary features from Athenaeus, and argue from Aeschylus and you will get high marks as a thoughtful and budding thinker regarding Homer.

Learning is about thinking, and thinking is about being critical, not "critical" as in unkind, but critical in that you weigh ideas reliably and draw conclusions that are well founded.

Going to college, becoming an adult, and living life as a responsible individual is an opportunity to sophisticate your ability to think and reason. Professors, the media, authors, colleagues, and friends will present you with ideas, information, and opinions. Unless something is obvious—like a scientific law—don't assume anything of importance is as it is presented without checking it out for yourself. Ask, why? An inquiring mind seeks to know.

This chapter is about the Bible for two reasons: 1) No other book or piece of literature is criticized like the Bible.

Why is that?

2) No other book in the history of literature has been scrutinized, assessed, and studied like the Bible. There are more commentaries on the Bible than any other book, holy book, or subject. Many of the great western universities were founded on biblical principle: Harvard, Yale, Princeton, Dartmouth, to name a few. The Bible is the best-selling book of all time, has been translated into more languages than any other book, is by far the most heavily documented and attested book of all time, and is more diligently studied than any book.

Why is that?

Questions for Consideration

1. What's your opinion of the Bible? How was your opinion or perspective formed? Now that you've read this chapter, are there any adjustments necessary in your view of the Bible?

2. Why do you think the Bible, of all literary options, is the most criticized book in the history of literature?

3. Why would the famous universities mentioned have founded themselves upon biblical principles?

CHAPTER 8

READING THE BIBLE

If you've never read the Bible, let me offer some pointers: First, it is not ordered sequentially. In other words, it doesn't read like a novel from page 1 to page 1450. It's organized categorically and is a collection of sixty-six books, each with its own theme.

Second, it's got two parts: an old part and a new part, each called a testament. The two parts are quite different in style and most folks find that reading the new section first helps digest the old at a later reading.

Finally, there are numerous translations of the Bible, i.e. its original language is not English, and this can be overwhelming to sort out.

Years ago I had a friend—a Jewish man—who converted from Judaism to Christianity. One day he called: "Hey, I'm at the bookstore. Thought I'd buy a Bible. There's a whole wall of them! I don't get it. When I wanted a copy of the *Torah*, I went and bought a *Torah*. There was one to choose from. What the hell's with all these Bibles?"

Great question.

Let me recommend two translations to consider and one to avoid.

For a more traditional translation, I suggest the *English Standard Version*. For a more modern reading, I suggest *The Message*. You can't go wrong with either and both are readily available.

My advice is to stay away from the *New International Version*. It is a deeply flawed translation.

So, where to begin? I suggest you start with the Book of John, also known as the Gospel of John, in the New Testament. It's straightforward reading that will introduce you to Jesus' claims, the story of His life, and the importance of Him to you and you to Him. It will be listed in the Table of Contents.

The Bible is simple. In fact, it says that the message of Jesus Christ is so simple a child can grasp it. So, don't overthink what you read.

But realize as well, the Bible is also profound. In fact, you can devote your entire life to studying it and never plumb its depths. Millions have. Millions more will. I encourage you to be one of them.

Questions for Consideration

1. Why would the two parts of the Bible be labeled as testaments? A testament is synonymous with a covenant. Thoughts?

2. Why does it matter which translation of the Bible you read?

3. Preston suggested you begin reading in the Book of John. If you've started, what's your takeaway from Chapter 1 of John's book?

CHAPTER 9

HISTORY

"That which has been is that which will be, / And that which has been done is that which will be done, / So there is nothing new under the sun."[32]

"That which has been is far off, and deep, very deep; who can find it out?"[33]

These are the musings of the author of Ecclesiastes, generally recognized as the wisest man to ever live.

Years ago a group of parents decided to homeschool their children and asked if I would teach their 7th and 8th grade kids World History. I told them, "No." They persisted. I declined. One more time, with increased determination, they pressured me to guide their children through world affairs.

---

32 Ecclesiastes 1:9. NASB.

33 Ecclesiastes 7:24. ESV.

"Look, I appreciate you asking me. I really do. But I am not going to teach your kids history."

"Why not? Just give us a reason."

"Because I will require your kids to read and write. A lot. It will be hard. Demanding, even. They will have to defend their work—and I'm relentless. I will force them to think, assess, and question."

It never fazed them. "Not a problem. We want them to read and write. We want you to teach them."

Finally: "Look, history is about money, power, and sex. I'm not going to teach your children about sex."

The parents quickly committed themselves, "Oh! No problem. We'll tell our kids about sex before you start classes."

So, I agreed. And, the parents told their kids [more] about sex. To be clear, the kids already knew where babies came from, and were aware of sexual attraction, but how the power of sexuality influenced history was new information.

Money? Power? Sex? Our examination of history was unvarnished.

Humanity routinely operates at the lowest common denominators—money, power, and sex—not that there's anything wrong with any of the three, but it's important to realize the underlying drivers when you consider history.

You've heard the truism, "Follow the money." Well, it's true. It doesn't matter if it's Congress, your school, or your church. If you need to know, follow the money.

For insights into power, observe those entrusted with some. Most folks will do anything to gain and retain power. It's intoxicating. It's addicting. It's also corrupting. Lord Acton said, "Power tends to corrupt and absolute power corrupts absolutely."[34] Lewis said it like this, "It is the magician's bargain: give up our soul, get power in return. But once our souls, that is, ourselves, have been given up, the power thus conferred will not belong to us. We shall in fact be the slaves and puppets of that to which we have given our souls."[35]

As to sex, recall the test question: What started World War I? The desired answer is that World War I started because Archduke Ferdinand was assassinated in Sarajevo, Bosnia. But seriously? He was an obscure, lower-level diplomat.

The definitive book on World War I is by Barbara Tuchman, *The Guns of August*.[36] You should read it. World War I occurred because of elaborate regional alliances based upon powerful marriages (sex).

There are two more things you should understand about history.

First, history is not simply facts and dates. History contains these, but history is the story of people.

I used to tell my students, "I don't care if you can tell me when the War of 1812 occurred. What I'm interested in you understanding is why the war occurred and what transpired in the lives of people and nations as a result."

---

34 Acton Institute. "Acton Research: Lord Acton Quote Archive." *Acton.org.* <https://www.acton.org/research/lord-acton-quote-archive>. Accessed, 21 April 2020.

35 Lewis, C.S. *The Abolition of Man.* P. 72.

36 Tuchman, Barbara W. *The Guns of August.* Random House. New York, NY. 1962, 2014.

My reason for wanting this for my students leads me into the second thing you should understand about history: If you don't understand your history, you are destined to repeat your history.[37]

Here's a possible—and troubling—case in point: As I write to you, America is reconsidering the history of its most costly war, the Civil War. It's doing so reactively, simplistically, and without much foresight or reflection.

Depending on how you look at the numbers, about the same number of Americans died in the Civil War as have died *cumulative* in all its subsequent wars. Per capita, if the war occurred today, 6,000,000 to 7,000,000 Americans would die, about 2% of the population.[38] Said another way, "The Civil War's rate of death, its incidence in comparison with the size of the American population, was six times that of World War II."[39]

This is an astounding amount of death and dying and suffering.

What's concerning is that our current actions indicate a failure—perhaps an unwillingness—to understand, grasp, or grapple with the lessons of our national history from 1850-1880. This is troubling, especially since our current period of time most closely parallels our nation's history leading up to the Civil War, 1850-1861.

---

37 Edmund Burke (1729-1797) first stated this truism. Many others have made the same observation: George Santayana, Steve Barry, Paul Christopher, Cynthia Patterson, Jesse Ventura, et al.

38 Ancestry. "12 Stunning Civil War Facts." *Ancestry.com.* May 21, 2014. <https://blogs.ancestry.com/cm/12-stunning-civil-war-facts/>. Accessed, 1 May 2020.

39 Faust, Drew Gilpin. "Death and Dying." *NPS.gov.* <https://www.nps.gov/nr/travel/national_cemeteries/Death.html>. Accessed, 4 July 2020.

If we don't understand our history, we are in danger of repeating our history.

"Approximately one in four soldiers that went to war never returned home."[40] Somewhere between 620,000 to 750,000 soldiers died during the war.[41] Of these, around 40,000 were black.[42] Twice as many soldiers died from disease as from battle wounds.[43] Civilian casualties are estimated at 50,000.[44] Historian James McPherson "…has concluded that the overall mortality rate for the South exceeded that of any country in World War I and all but the region between the Rhine and the Volga in World War II."[45]

Did all these, our forebearers, die in vain?

I fear a less-than-thoughtful, simplistic reduction of history, may indicate they did. It is not unreasonable to listen to what these people tell us from their graves, but digesting their perspectives is complicated. Calling each other ugly names and denouncing those with a differing opinion is not only counterproductive, it is dangerous.

---

40 American Battlefield Trust. "Civil War Casualties." *Battlefields.org.* <https://www.battlefields.org/learn/articles/civil-war-casualties>. Accessed, 1 May 2020.

41 Gugliotta, Guy. "New Estimate Raises Civil War Death Toll." *NYTimes.com.* April 2, 2012. <https://www.nytimes.com/2012/04/03/science/civil-war-toll-up-by-20-percent-in-new-estimate.html>. Accessed, 4 July 2020.

42 *History.com.* "Black Civil War Soldiers." June 7, 2019. < https://www.history.com/topics/american-civil-war/black-civil-war-soldiers>. Accessed, 4 July 2020.

43 Faust, Drew Gilpin. Ibid.

44 Ibid.

45 Ibid.

Some history is simple. Most history is complex. Approaching your history simplistically will generally result in a repeat of the lesson to be learned.

History is a message from the dead past to the living present. Historian and writer David McCullough said, "History is a guide to navigation in perilous times. History is who we are and why we are the way we are."[46]

Given this, i.e. that history is about us and perilous times, then history is a voice from our ancestors offering counsel to us. Hearing and listening can afford a remarkable advantage to us who are living. General Mattis says, "Living in history builds your own shock absorber, because you'll learn that there are lots of old solutions to new problems."[47]

People are complex. You are complex. In fact, you are so complex there never has nor ever will be another you. Cultures, societies, countries—the more people within a group, the more complex analysis becomes. Add duress—famine, war, revolution, disease, genocide, time, enslavement—and complexity grows exponentially. This is the challenge of history. This is the demand upon those who consider it.

What's the point of this chapter?

I'm hoping to help you conceptualize what history is and how to responsibly consider its guidance and record. The next time you hear someone explain a

---

46 McCullough, David. Quoted in "The New York Times" from his commencement speech to Wesleyan University. "Historian Addresses Wesleyan." *NYTimes.com*. June 4, 1984. <https://www.nytimes.com/1984/06/04/nyregion/historian-addresses-wesleyan.html>. Accessed, 12 June 2020.

47 Mattis, James N. Ibid. P. 237.

war, or a period, or a people, or an epoch in a simple statement, an offhanded comment, or a categorical summary, be suspicious. History is rarely simple because people are not simple.

Reject simplistic perspectives. Go look for yourself. Anything less is neither self-respecting nor respectful of humanity and our historical record.

Questions for Consideration

1. History is about sex, money, and power—not the details of the Treaty of Versailles, per se. This means history is about people. How does this definition of history change your view of history?

2. Does knowing the underpinnings of history make it more relevant for you? In other words, the same things drove history during the Byzantine Empire that drive history today. What's your takeaway knowing this?

3. Agree or disagree: Reducing significant historical events to media soundbites and simplistic explanations will eventually compromise our ability to make progress and destine us to repeat history in some form or fashion? And—you knew this follow-up was coming—why are you of the opinion you just decided upon?

Chapter 10

CAUSE AND EFFECT

In October 1974, Billy Preston sang, "Nothin' from nothin' leaves nothin'."[48] The song topped the charts for several months.

He was singing about what it takes to have a meaningful relationship, but the catch phrase also offers important wisdom for how we are currently thinking.

Philosophy speaks of first causes. By this, philosophers are pointing to the lowest common denominator, the fundamental principle, the root idea— the absolute necessity of identifying the starting point. You've got to have something before you can have anything. Nothing cannot yield something.

It's a rudimentary point. Almost not worth making it's so obvious.

---

48 Preston, Billy. "Nothing from Nothing." *The Kids and Me*. A&M Records. Santa Monica, CA. 1974.

Yet, push an evolutionist backward, farther and farther in evolutionary theory, and he eventually confronts some version of a primordial ooze where bacteria form up and begin ascending the evolutionary ladder. But where did the ooze come from? How did the first bacterium happen to become? And the second?

Astronomers fill books with formulas for the Big Bang. Go online and search "Big Bang" and fantastic images created by computer models show how it happened. Molecules, fission, fusion, gravity, explosions—it's totally cool stuff.

But where did the original material come from? Stephen Hawking, the late acclaimed physicist, concludes in his book, *The Grand Design*, that gravity made the original material: "Because there is a law such as gravity, the universe can and will create itself from nothing."[49]

The astronomer thinking about big things has the same problem the evolutionist does who's thinking about incredibly small things.

What was the first thing? What cause prompted the first effect?

What you decide the first cause is, or how the first thing came about, leaves a number of options. You can say that God exists and that He produced the first thing. The more politically savory expression of this is termed intelligent design.

---

49 Gabbatt, Adam. "Stephen Hawking Says Universe Not Created by God." *TheGuardian.com.* September 1, 2010. <https://www.theguardian.com/science/2010/sep/02/stephen-hawking-big-bang-creator>. Accessed, 5 May 2020.

Any of these are fine starting points because they acknowledge you have to have something before you can have anything.

It's such a simple truth. What accounts then for wholesale denial of cause and effect?

I don't believe it has anything to do with logic or rationality. I believe the denial has to do with the existence of God—by whatever name you wish to call Him. As nearly as I can tell, there are only two options: 1) denial of God's existence as well as first things, or 2) recognition of God as the originator of first things.

Choosing denial forces you to arbitrarily start an elaborate, rational, wildly complex, creative process on the basis of an impossibility. But if you choose to recognize the existence of God, then intellectual honesty insists that you bow your knee to God.

It's a tough choice for independent souls, but it's one or the other.

As you listen to these two options play out in daily life, pay attention to what's being said. Sooner or later, an honest conversation grapples with the two options. A rational discussion that veers into irrationality regarding cause and effect indicates the presenter dodged God—and the first thing—in order to maintain personal independence. That's their prerogative, but let's be honest about what transpired.

Fundamentally, there must be a cause to have an effect. This means where the first cause[50] came from is important and must be answered. Otherwise, your foundational beliefs are tenuous.

---

50 Thomas Aquinas (1225-1274), an Italian philosopher, formulated five proofs for the existence of God by reasoning from the cosmos backward. I'm relying heavily in this footnote on R.C. Sproul's, *The Consequences of Ideas*, pp. 70-74. Most of what follows is his, edited by me for brevity, but without the customary quote marks and ellipses in an effort to make the note more readable and approachable.

Aquinas' first reason had to do with the law of motion. Whatever is moved must be moved by some prior actuality. But this change, the movement, cannot regress to infinity, because in that case the motion could never begin. Therefore, Aquinas concludes, there must be a first mover.

Second, he reasons from the law of causality. No event can be its own cause. Every event requires a prior cause. Every prior cause must have its own cause. At some point the series must end. It's impossible to regress to infinity, as the idea of an infinite regress involves the notion of a causeless effect, an absurdity infinitely compounded.

Third, he reasons from necessary being. If there was a time when nothing existed, then nothing could ever start to exist and nothing would exist now. But if something *does* exist now, there must have always been something in existence; something must exist that possesses *necessary* existence–its existence is not merely possible but necessary.

Aquinas' fourth line of reasoning is from comparison. We are aware that there are degrees of good, noble, and true, but something can be deemed good or true only against some maximum norm or standard. We can't have a relative good or relative truth unless the relative is measured against an absolute. There must be something which is to all beings the cause of their being, goodness, and every other perfection.

His fifth reason proceeds from the evidence of order in the universe. We observe in nature things that lack intelligence but function in an orderly and purposive way, e.g. the seeds of a dandelion cast in the wind are designed for the plant's reproduction, but the plant lacks any intelligence to think about this or plan for it to occur. There is obvious design and order–and design requires a designer. Things lacking intelligence cannot act in a designed fashion unless they are first directed by something that does have intelligence. An arrow does not guide itself to the target unless it is first aimed there by the archer.

Additionally, things cannot be directed to their ends by chance. Chance can direct nothing, because chance can do nothing. Chance can do nothing because chance is nothing. Chance has no being, and that which has no being has no power to do anything.

In short, philosophers lump Aquinas' reasoning into the term, necessary self-existence, or just self-existence.

Questions for Consideration

1. Our philosophers tell us, nothing cannot yield something. Stephen Hawking, a physicist, was of the opinion that gravity created the beginning of the universe. What do you think?

2. What do you believe was the first cause?

3. Philosophers recognize the rule of first cause. Many scientists do not. What requires you to think either philosophically or scientifically? What would an eclectic approach look like?

Chapter 11

GENERALITIES

For years, I drank Scotch most Monday evenings with my atheist neighbor. We talked about everything—and I mean everything.

I knew the importance of ensuring clear communication, but those years visiting with my neighbor reinforced the importance of not assuming, dispensing with lingo not common to us both, e.g. Christian-speak, and not speaking in abstract generalities.

Thinking about generalities in particular, my neighbor had little patience for an abstraction. When I made such a *faux pas* (mistake), he would wave his hands in the air dismissively, interrupt me, "Preston, descend the abstraction."

Meaning: Get rid of the assumptions, lingo, generalizations, dependent statements, and tell me what you are saying—straight up, just the nub of the idea all by itself. If the statement won't stand on its own without props, then it is presumably a false statement. On the other hand, if a statement has standing, i.e. the idea is legitimate, then you can begin testing, or discussing, or exploring the solid premise it contains.

In important matters, it is essential for clear understanding that you work your way backward until you find the starting point, the genesis, the fundamental idea. Then you can have a meaningful conversation that solves problems, builds understanding, and advances ideas.

Once upon a time, I landed on the Finance Committee at my church. The economy was bad, donations were down, expenses were up, the budget was a wreck, everyone was stressed.

The pastor dropped in on one of our meetings, which was not normal, so it was obvious he had something on his mind for the committee. He was a good man, and a good minister, and he was dying a slow and horrid death by cancer. He looked like hell. When he sat down, he didn't sit; he dropped. His eyes were hollow, his skin gray, his voice hoarse, his white hair had turned yellow and thin. Whew.

His idea was a building project to modify how the auditorium of the church joined the fellowship hall and nursery. It was a good idea that resolved numerous bad architectural realities. Every person on the committee wanted to honor the pastor in his dying days—and it was clear, the building project was his dying desire.

Billy, who's gone now, but who spent his professional life engineering highway projects around the Great State of Texas, spoke after a time. He was genteel. Leaning his 6'4" body forward while simultaneously uncrossing his legs and putting both cowboy boots on the floor, he attempted to not be intimidating. He said, "Pastor, it's a grand idea. We all agree. How do you propose to pay for it?"

The pastor sat forward also. He presented his idea all over again, but with more compulsion in his second telling.

Carefully, gently, quietly Billy asked again, "Pastor, how do you propose that the church pay for this project?"

The pastor began a third time. Stopped. Looked at each member of the committee, clasped his hands, and said, "I don't know."

Now, everyone at the table knew what we were dealing with: An abstract, good idea that lacked realistic funding during a budgetary shortfall.

There was nothing wrong with the minister's idea. It achieved all kinds of advantageous outcomes. Billy's question wasn't heavy-handed and the position of the committee wasn't recalcitrant or obstructionist. In fact, as I write to you my stomach is roiling with the recall of that awful, tragic, terrible moment when the abstract, general idea of a building project succumbed to the harsh reality of our P&L's (profit and loss statement) bottom line.

I won't leave you hanging: The building project happened, but not before the pastor died. In the end, his idea became a better plan, a larger plan, a project we paid for in cash, with a fellowship hall named after our deceased minister.

This was a superior outcome to taking on debt for a good idea that we couldn't pay for because we reacted to the emotional appeal of a dying man instead of looking hard at our financial reality.

Whether building a building, paying for nationalized healthcare, comprehending evolution, grasping prayer without ceasing,[51] having an argument, or planning your vacation, things will go better for you (and all concerned) if you descend the abstraction of an idea until the generalities become concrete, objective fundamentals.

Working to start from—or locate—the beginning is what's called active listening, or active conversation. You achieve this by implementing linguistic tools that seek to understand:

- "Tell me more about that, please."

- "How did that make you feel?"

- "If I understand correctly, you are saying (and you repeat back what you heard)."

This linguistic technique facilitates mutual respect between yourself and another. With this mutual generosity, active dialogue can occur and is wildly beneficial.

I communicate like this with my wife and friends. Candidly, I actively communicate with myself when I'm by myself. If I can't readily work my way back to a solid starting point in my thoughts, I retreat to my journal and write it out seeking to discover the kinds of information the bullet points above seek.

---

51 Cf.: 1 Thessalonians 5:17. NASB.

When you're listening to a lecture, reading a book, considering an idea, discussing issues within a work group—or talking with your friend, listening to your pastor, reading the Bible, or just pondering what comes next—seek diligently to identify the nub of the idea. Stay at it until the abstraction is no longer abstract but concrete. Starting points are foundations and foundations must be solid or what follows is unreliable.

In discussing faith with my atheist neighbor, we finally found our way to the nub of faith—or, almost the nub. As I was leaving one Monday evening, he put his arm over my shoulder and said, "Preston, let's face it: You took a leap of faith and I took a leap of unfaith, yet we are the best of friends."

It was a touching affirmation—that I let lie for that evening. My neighbor's notion of a leap was an abstraction to avoid a demanding reality—a complex form of justification and denial.

Where did he leap from, and what did he leap to in his mind, and over what distance, and what hurdles?

The next Monday, after catching up, I revisited my neighbor's leap of unfaith. I came at it this way: "You know, we should quantify how large the leap is we each took." He cocked his head and lifted his right eyebrow. I said, "In the end, if I'm wrong about my faith, what have I lost?" I shrugged. "Nothing really. My leap was inconsequential. But in the end, if you are wrong in your unfaith, the leap you took is astronomical."

My neighbor's atheism was now quantified. As we visited, he and I could use the same measuring stick and measure the distance, cost, and risk of his unfaith and my faith.

My neighbor's atheism was now clear. It had little to do with doubt and everything to do with a decision against belief. By quantifying the leap, his atheism was clear. It wasn't so much intellectual as it was a wild gamble.

And, that's fine. It's his decision in the end.

What was important was to descend the abstractions of faith and atheism until we determined what faith required and what was at stake, and what atheism required and what was at stake.

As my neighbor said, "Preston, you took a [small] leap of faith and I took a [monstrous] leap of unfaith."

Questions for Consideration

1. What do you believe Preston's neighbor meant when he said, "Descend the abstraction"?

2. What makes the questions Preston recommends powerful tools for defining generalities?

3. What made Preston's leap of faith a small generality and his neighbor's leap of unfaith a monstrous generality?

CHAPTER 12

GOOD

There are people in this world who are deranged psychopaths, souls who are out of touch with reality, society, and themselves. At the extreme, these folks are also out of touch with good and evil, moral and immoral, right and wrong.

But I'm not here to write about psychopaths. I'm here to write to you, a normal person.

You understand good versus evil. It's innate within you. I'm not talking about right versus wrong. You don't automatically sense right from wrong or you would never make a mistake.

But a sense of good is innate—no one has to tell you what is good. Thus, the question: How do you automatically know what is good?

Before we consider this question, let's first work backward: There is evil in this world. Again, unless you are out of touch with reality, there is no question among you and your friends that evil exists.

This merits the question: "How do you know what evil is?"

And the simple answer is, "It's obvious."

What I'm getting at is how do you recognize that evil is evil? And you say, "Because it is the opposite of good. When I see evil, I know it is not good."

Now we are back where we began: How do you know what good is?

It's like an absolute standard of good exists. By it, you and perhaps all people, innately recognize good from evil.

Where did good come from? How did good come to be in the first place? Where did the standards defining good originate? Who established the standard for good—a standard so noble and clear we all recognize it?

If good didn't just occur—it's been here all along—then something that knows good, or is good, had to establish it and make it absolute in the world. And whoever or whatever did this has to be absolutely and naturally good, all the time, in every way, regardless of all other forces that might come to bear.

I don't know if Plato (429-347 BCE) was the first person to think about absolute good or not. But, he was the first person to write about it. He examined the existence of good from every angle and identified what he termed the "the Idea of the Good."

Numerous later thinkers, especially Christian thinkers, ridiculed Plato for not labeling his Idea of Good as "God." But Plato wasn't looking for God, per se. He was exploring the world of thought, rationality, and reason. The Idea of Good was as far as his rational mind would or could reason.

The "God step" required faith. Plato was interested in reason, not faith.[52]

However, while Plato did not call his Idea of Good, God, he did identify the Idea of Good as supreme, i.e. superior to the Greek pantheon of gods and all the other gods he identified, e.g. the sun, and declared that everything divine was born from the Idea of Good.

Plato went on to conclude that absolute goodness, his Idea of Good, must come to us and make itself known. In other words, private or distant or disengaged goodness is less than good, flawed by remaining separate from mankind, and thus not totally good.

That we know good from evil indicates that Plato was right. Good has come to us. We recognize it.

While speaking with a rich man who called him "Good Teacher," Jesus identified absolute goodness as residing in God alone. That the rich man called Jesus, Good Teacher, indicates he recognized Jesus as God and the embodiment of absolute goodness. Jesus did not tell the man he was mistaken.[53]

---

52 This is not to say Plato thought faith was irrational. Faith compliments reason and vice versa.

53 Mark 10:17-18. NASB.

Remarkably, Plato lived four centuries before Jesus Christ. But clearly he anticipated what we term, the Incarnation, i.e. the coming of God in Jesus Christ (i.e. what we celebrate at Christmas), the goodness of God in human form.

Had Plato lived to see the first Christmas, it's reasonable to suspect he would have named his Idea of Good, "God," because he would have identified his Idea of Good doing exactly what he knew absolute goodness must do to be totally good: come to us.[54]

The message of Christianity is that God continues to come to us—in zillions of ways, throughout all our days, to each one of us whether Believer or unbeliever. It's what God does because it is the perfect expression of good.[55]

We are free to recognize the origin of our idea of good or not. Just because God comes to us doesn't mean we must believe. We are still the beneficiaries of goodness.

But if opting for unbelief, it seems to me that before the existence of God can be dismissed, there must first be an accounting for how good and the universal knowledge of it came to be.

---

54 Plato spoke and wrote in Koine Greek, the same dialect spoken by Alexander the Great, Jesus, and the writers of the New Testament of the Bible. Unlike English, Greek utilizes three genders: masculine (he), feminine (she), and neuter (it). Plato's "the Idea of the Good" uses the neuter gender for "the good." Thus, four paragraphs earlier, I use "itself" (neuter) to modify "good." In the paragraph describing Jesus' conversation with the rich man, I note Mark 10:17-18. This exchange appears also in Matthew and Luke. In Matthew 19:17, the grammar is similar in use to Plato's. In this passage, Jesus changes the gender of "good" from neuter to masculine. At first, He uses the neuter when asking, "Why do you ask me about what is good (neuter)?" He answers His question using the masculine gender: "There is only one who is good (masculine)." It could be argued from the Mark passage that the gender change is inconsequential. However, it could be argued from the Matthew passage that Jesus was personalizing "the one who is good," i.e. putting a face on Plato's idea and implying that the good had come and was humanly present. It's not a definitive argument, but neither is it one to be categorically dismissed.

55 Romans 1:20; Job 12:7-10; Psalm 19:1-6. NASB.

Questions for Consideration

1. What is necessary to have a concept of what constitutes, or defines, the concept of good?

2. What do you believe Plato meant by what he termed, the Idea of Good?

3. What is Plato's logic for saying that if the Idea of Good is absolutely good, then it is required to make itself known—to come down—to mankind?

Chapter 13

APOLOGETICS

An apologetic is a defense. The dictionary puts it this way: reasoned arguments in justification of something.

When I was in high school, I heard about a book on Christian apologetics by Josh McDowell, *Evidence That Demands a Verdict*. I bought a copy and sat down to read.

Except, it wasn't readable.

Forgive me if you know this, but before internet search engines existed, you had to go to the library to conduct research. Literally, you looked through a card catalog organized by subjects—like a miniature file cabinet—found a possible source, went to that area of the library, located the book you wanted, scanned the pages to find any relevant piece of information to your project, and if successful, then transcribed this information by hand onto an index card to be used later in composing your research paper. Today, you query online databases.

McDowell's book was a collection of research cards, organized by subject, and bound together with a cover. Each entry was self-contained. It was readable like the dictionary is readable. I realized I had purchased a compilation of sources, not a piece of literature, and that it contained important information—if I could figure out how to utilize it.

Such was my introduction to Christian apologetics, i.e. a defense of the key elements of Christian faith and belief. Today, there are readable sources—lots of them—as well as thousands of audio and video sources. I've included a few recommendations in the back of *Swagger*.

My undergraduate degree is in antiquities, i.e. ancient history, from Missouri State University. My classes usually began with the beginnings of civilization in the Tigris and Euphrates Rivers area and progressed through the centuries until stopping around 100 CE (also, AD), part way through the Roman Empire. There are lots of works of antiquity. You probably had to read *The Gilgamesh Epic* at some point. But in terms of ancient artifacts, by far the most complete work of ancient history is the Bible. Consequently, the Bible was a required book in all my classes.

When I first saw the Bible on my required book's list, I was thrilled. I grew up in a Christian home, was taken to church every time the doors were open, and was a committed follower of Jesus Christ. I was well-versed about my Bible, knew chapter and verse, and could proficiently answer the questions at Sunday School.

Missouri State University was not a Christian college. The study of ancient history was not Sunday School. If my professors were Christians, I couldn't discern it.

I was totally unprepared for critiques of the Bible's legitimacy, veracity, and viability. In nearly every class, the default disposition of the professor was anti-Bible. Every lecture assumed the Bible's fallibility for every reason known to man. If it wasn't contradictory, then it wasn't dated correctly. If it presented something as true, there was another source presented as preferable. The sources used by my professors were unknown to me. The approach was scholarly, not theological.

After a few months of this degree program, I was punch-drunk. My faith was frazzled. My Bible was unraveling. My spiritual confidence was on the floor.

Came the day, sitting in Dr. Moyer's class, a scholar with a double doctorate, where I concluded, *I can't do this anymore. Something is wrong. I don't know what it is, but everything I believe is up for grabs. I've got to get this figured out.* As I sat listening to Dr. Moyer—a truly wonderful prof, by the way—I determined a course of action: I would attend classes and go to work (I was a janitor), but all other time would be spent in the library until I resolved my beliefs about Christianity and the Bible.

As soon as Dr. Moyer released us, I was in the library.

It took about two weeks of study, combing through sources, comparing perspectives, and so forth before I resolved my doubts.

I learned that there are always two sides to everything. For each source questioning the Bible's reliability, there was an equally respected source saying the opposite. If one source pronounced the Bible contradictory, another dispelled that criticism and demonstrated its cohesion.

As I wrote in the chapter about the Bible, I also realized that a number of primary sources in the study of antiquities—in the zeal to be empirical—held ancient writers accountable to modern standards and judged their legitimacy accordingly. Ramm writes, "Rationalism in Biblical studies boils down to the fundamental assertion that whatever is not in harmony with *educated* mentality is to be rejected."[56]

The dice were loaded. The deck stacked. These scholars could always win and sound intellectual and the Bible would always lose. The scholarly playing field wasn't level; it was contrived. Because the Bible was not written to modern standards, because it is metaphysical, not scientific, it was deemed a flawed collection of myths—and if Christianity's holy book is myth, Christianity is mythological and irrational.

Sproul writes, "Christianity may contain mystery and paradox, but it is not irrational. If the leap of faith is a leap into the absurd, it is fatal. Scripture calls us to leap out of the darkness into the light—it is not a leap into the darkness where one hopes that God is waiting with a net."[57]

---

56 Ramm, Bernard. *Protestant Biblical Interpretation*. Baker Book House. Grand Rapids, MI. 1970. P. 63.

57 Sproul, R.C. *The Consequences of Ideas*. Crossway. Wheaton, IL. 2000. P. 157.

Since the Bible is the most complete and attested book of antiquity, it is therefore the most lauded, examined, and the most criticized book of antiquity. Let's face it, even if you believe the Bible is divinely inspired, it will fall apart—become mythological and irrational—when held to a standard that didn't exist at the time of its writing.

I departed the library one night at closing—midnight I think—and walked across campus in a falling snow. My faith was secured. I understood how to think my way through the Bible—or at least well enough to maintain my intellectual footing. I knew how to manage contradictory sources. It was a huge relief, although I spent the rest of the semester catching up on all the papers and reading I'd let go while I studied other things.

I didn't quite correlate my library adventure to apologetics, but that's what I was doing, i.e. figuring out whether or not what I believed was defensible.

My program required that I read and write a lot. Each research project had to include both sides of an argument. Of course, I referenced what this archaeologist said differently from that archaeologist, but I also integrated research from McDowell's book of apologetic research. What I found interesting is that the only source I ever quoted that a professor took issue with was McDowell, and I quoted from hundreds of sources.

It caught me by surprise. Why is the source from McDowell not a reliable or acceptable source?

In the end, I determined it wasn't the source, it was the perspective of the source. If the Bible is more than a book of myths,[58] if it is a special book, truly unique, and inspired, then it is unlike any other book. While permissible, it is not a sensible option to read it and lay it aside. If it is what it purports to be, the inspired word of God, then it must be contended with, considered, and either embraced or rejected.

It took a long time for me to conclude how I feel about apologetics. My use of McDowell was good for me and my integrity as a Christian, but it consistently garnered me arbitrary red marks, dressing down, and intellectual suspicion.

The absence of fairness, tolerance, and understanding were an affront, but they forced me to engage apologetics. The study taught me to research, reason, and think. I'd like to believe you are the beneficiary of my lesson so many years ago.

Regardless of the subject in question, engage an apologetic endeavor. It's intellectually honest to do so, disingenuous to not do so. Stay with it until you are convinced.

---

58 Attaching the term "myth" to the Bible was disconcerting to me—and it was constant in my university degree program. At the time, my understanding of the word was that it applied to fables, Greek mythology, and stories that had a moral point but didn't really happen. "The Boy Who Cried Wolf" is a good example. There's a clear moral to the story, but listeners understand there is no literal boy who cried "wolf" three times. In my experience, how someone uses the word "myth" requires clarification. At its most basic, the definition of myth is synonymous with story. The definition offers no judgment about whether the story is true or if it is fiction. My professors referred to all stories of antiquity as myths. I never could discern whether that meant fact or fable, story or tall tale. To say the Bible is filled with stories is accurate. To say the Bible is myth requires additional information. If by this, the speaker or writer means the Bible is filled with stories, great. If he means the Bible is filled with stories on par with Greek mythology, I'm not fine.

Questions for Consideration

1. What is meant by the term, "apologetics"?

2. Have you been in a situation where your belief system was challenged, or felt broken, or undermined? When and why and what did you do in response?

3. Sproul is quoted: "Christianity may contain mystery and paradox, but it is not irrational. If the leap of faith is a leap into the absurd, it is fatal." Contrast this with the proclamation Preston's neighbor used to make that, "Religion makes people crazy." Who's right and who's wrong and why?

CHAPTER 14

DISTANT OR ENGAGED

When John F. Kennedy was President, he hosted the Nobel Prize dinner of 1962. The room was filled with the most intelligent people on the planet. In his opening remarks, he said, "I think this is the most extraordinary collection of talent, of human knowledge, that has ever been gathered together at the White House, with the possible exception of when Thomas Jefferson dined alone."[59]

In actuality, President Jefferson rarely dined alone, but that wasn't President Kennedy's point. He was conveying Jefferson's brilliance as well as a measure of humility for the honored guests.

---

59 Thomas Jefferson Foundation. "Extract from John F. Kennedy's Remarks at a Dinner Hosting Nobel Prize Winners of the Western Hemisphere." *Tjrs.monticello.org*. 2020. <http://tjrs.monticello.org/letter/1856>. Accessed, 22 April 2020.

Thomas Jefferson may be the world's most famous deist. In addition to legitimizing deism by his extraordinary intelligence, those claiming deism for themselves are often comforted that they too are intelligent—by inference.

Of course, believing the same thing Jefferson believed because he was an intelligent man doesn't make you intelligent. It makes you lazy.

Deism: This is a term you need to know.

Dictionary.com defines deism this way: "Belief in a God who created the world but has since remained indifferent to it.[60] So, creation administers itself through natural laws.

In Jefferson's case, he "…went through the Gospels (i.e. the biblical books of Matthew, Mark, Luke, and John) picking out the ethical and moral, and rejecting the theological. Once done, he published his *Jefferson Bible*."[61] Peter Manseau, a curator at the Smithsonian, is of the opinion that Jefferson saw Scripture as similar to a modern-day monument, "one he hoped not to destroy, but simply to cut down to size." Jefferson's completed work "…is a slim assemblage of about 1,000 verses, …a uniquely American testament shorn of its miraculous and supernatural elements, a Bible the sage of Monticello (i.e. Jefferson) could believe in without qualifications."[62]

---

60 Dictionary.com. "Deism." *Dictionary.com*. 2020. <https://www.dictionary.com/browse/deism>. Accessed, 22 April 2020.

61 Ramm, Bernard. Ibid. P. 69.

62 Manseau, Peter. "We Can Tear Down False Idols of History. Thomas Jefferson Did it to Jesus Christ." *WashingtonPost.com*. August 13, 2020. <https://www.washingtonpost.com/outlook/2020/08/13/jefferson-bible-remove-statues/>. Accessed, August 14, 2020.

Deism exists because people can't, won't, or haven't done the labor to connect God actively to life—assuming that's possible. Because there are hard questions in life, like how can a good God allow suffering, it seems easier and more rational to presume God is distant than work to reconcile how a good God engages in a world that convulses with ubiquitous pain and evil. Tozer writes, "Left to ourselves we tend immediately to reduce God to manageable terms."[63]

If God is good, as He claims to be, then deism is impossible. If God is good, His goodness requires that He engage with us—as Plato put it, that He come to us.

If God is distant, then He is not good. That makes His claim of goodness false and Him a lying, duplicitous fraud.

The Bible says many things about God, but the most profound occurs during the phenomenal exchange between God and Moses. As they are speaking about Moses going to Egypt to lead Israel out of bondage, Moses asks God what His name is. God replies, "I AM."[64]

God's an all-present, all-encompassing noun and verb simultaneously. To grasp Him on His terms requires both recognizing Him as God and embracing Him as active in your life. God is. God is being.

---

63 Tozer, A.W. *The Knowledge of the Holy.* HarperOne, a division of HarperCollins. New York, NY. 1961. P. 8.

64 Exodus 3:14. NASB. (Note: The capitalization is meant to more accurately translate the original Hebrew text.)

Hard to fathom, isn't it? Harder yet to reconcile how He is engaged when there is so much wrong.

Start thinking about this while mired in the muck of unsavory circumstance, with nothing but your intellect to guide your conclusion, and you wind up with Jefferson: God must be distant because you can't reconcile Him to your situation. If this is the case, clearly you are on your own.

Deistic thinking leads to this outcome: One of these days, you'll see this distant God, and when you do, you'd better be able to give a good account of yourself in all the circumstances of your life.

Given this, if you're smart, you'll vow to try hard. You'll be moral. You'll do right, because one of these days, there's going to be hell to pay with God for all your failings. Surely, there is less hell to pay for those who try hard to be good and moral than for those who don't.

In other words, deism believes in a God who can be offended—put off, distanced—by your shortfalls, or mine, or by crime, or racism, or inequity, or bigotry, or by any ill you want to name on this planet, and who expects a man to atone for his faults, and who will require that His justice be satisfied by the bad man reaping punishment and the good man reaping reward.

In short, deism believes in karma,[65] not God.

---

65 Wikipedia.org. "Karma." *Wikipedia.org.* 2020. <https://en.wikipedia.org/wiki/Karma>. Accessed, 22 April 2020. Karma means action, work, or deed. It refers to the spiritual principle that what you do in this life has cause and effect in this life and in your future existence. Do good here, reap happiness now and in the future. Do evil here, reap evil and unhappiness later.

This deistic view is not Jefferson's alone. Descartes, Spinoza, Fontenelle, Voltaire, Rousseau—and many, many more to this day—each saw God as distant and man left to his own resourcefulness.

A close friend, age 47, three young kids, a spectacular wife, a great career, was diagnosed with liver cancer. It metastasized. Chemo. Radiation. He couldn't eat. Couldn't poop. Couldn't burp. He felt like he would explode. It was horrid. He couldn't reconcile abandoning his young family due to death-by-cancer with a God who was present—actually, a God who didn't answer his prayers for healing. He didn't declare himself a deist, but when God didn't do what he wanted, he lived deism.

When King George VI asked Prime Minister Winston Churchill about his family, Churchill replied, "My father was like God—busy elsewhere."[66]

Casting God in an image we conceive seems easier in the moment, especially a tumultuous moment, than to embrace the God who is and figure out what His constant presence means. It is easier to define God by activity we attribute to Him than by who He says He is.

Saying that God is the God of creation is inaccurate, inadequate, and shortsighted, not to mention wrong. The Christian God does not exist because there is a creation. Saying this makes Him a principle, a function. It makes Him the Author of Nature. But He is a stillborn God if that is all He is.

---

66 Churchill, Winston. "The Darkest Hour." *IMDB.com*. 1990-2020. <https://www.imdb.com/title/tt4555426/quotes/qt3712840>. Accessed, 22 April 2020.

The God who is may create if He chooses, but the essence of who He is, is not to create, but to be: "I AM." He is saying, "I am constant being." The God who is cannot be distant, nor can He be boxed in by describing what He does, or boxed out because you can't reconcile your circumstance with His presence. Voltaire said, "In the beginning God created man in His own image, and man has been trying to return the favor ever since."[67]

Long before Thomas Jefferson, another famous deist, René Descartes (1596-1650), defined God—indeed, limited God—to what he believed God did in creation. Thus, Descartes' view of God was constrained by what he could observe. Pascal said, "I cannot forgive Descartes. In all his philosophy he would have been quite willing to dispense with God. But he had to make Him give a fillip to set the world in motion; beyond this, he had no further need of God."[68]

Struggling to comprehend how God engages is to be expected. You are not God. How can you be expected to fully understand His ways?

But to disengage God, or place Him in a distant heaven, and declare Him removed because you can't see Him is arrogant. In doing so, you adopt deism and cast aspersion on the goodness of God.

If He is not good, then He is not God.

---

67 Voltaire. *Goodreads.com*. 2020. <https://www.goodreads.com/quotes/801843-in-the-beginning-god-created-man-in-his-own-image>. Accessed, 22 April 2020.

68 Pascal, Blaise. *Pensees*. Translated by, W.F. Trotter. As quoted by, Etienne Gilson. *God and Philosophy*. Yale University Press. New Haven, CT. 1941. P. 88.

The god of deism is but a wraith of the living God. Many would argue that deism is simple atheism, i.e. atheism in disguise.

By definition, how God engages is not always obvious. Give God room to be God and be realistic enough to acknowledge that you are not. It is lazy, presumptuous, and self-important to assume that your lack of clarity means God is absent.

God is and He is good or He is not at all.

Therefore, He must be present and engaged—or not. Distant is not a rational option. It is an emotional, circumstantial reaction.

It is shortsighted and profoundly dangerous to assume circumstances in a flawed world render an accurate representation of God's engagement. You can't understand, know, or recognize God by studying circumstance. That's backward thinking. Rather, you manage your circumstantial outlook based upon what you know of the good God who is.

The primary means by which God is known is the Bible. He declares that He is love. He is good. He is just in all His ways. He loves what is right and He is always faithful.[69] That you can't always reconcile who He is to your circumstance says nothing of note about who God is, only that you are a human being with limited sight.

However, we are not blind and we need not be ignorant. There are discoverable answers to some of what plagues us in this life. When we read

---

69 Cf.: 1 John 4:7-21; John 3:16; Mark 10:17-18; Psalm 37:28; 33:5; 1 Corinthians 1:9; Galatians 5:22-23; 2 Thessalonians 3:3; 2 Timothy 2:13. NASB.

Mandela, Solzhenitsyn, Nee, Hugo's *Les Misérables*, or hear the outlook voiced by Malala, Churchill, FDR, King, Tada, and a host of others who have suffered trials, we gain some perspective regarding injustice and suffering, but questions remain. *C'est la vie*, such is life. One of these days, all that is lost will be found and all that is mystery will be revealed.

As nearly as I can determine, the trap Jefferson (and all deists) fell into was believing that he was smart enough, powerful enough, important enough— indeed arrogant enough, to assume he could comprehend and understand God within his own intellect and experience. When he couldn't, or couldn't reconcile what he assumed about God with what he observed in the world around him, rather than confess his human limitation and acknowledge God's sovereignty, he pronounced God distant, disengaged, and removed.

God is. He is engaged. He is big. He is powerful. He is all-present. He is active. He is good. How this works out is a lifetime of living, praying, and humbly calling upon God to overcome your unbelief and help you tap into your faith.[70]

Trusting yourself and your life to God is the humble acknowledgment that He is larger than you, knows more than you, sees more than you, is more powerful than you... and that you trust Him who is and who is good.[71]

In a world assaulting your senses with evil and wrong, the temptation is to conclude that circumstance tells you all there is to know, i.e. if God is not

---

70 Cf.: Mark 9:23-24. NASB.

71 Cf.: John 10:10; Ephesians 3:20-21; Job 38:1-42:6. NASB.

observable by whatever measure, then He must be absent. You may as well dispatch the *Holy Bible* and do your best with the *Jefferson Bible*.

It is impossible for the God who is to leave you alone, i.e. not be present. It is your prerogative to do with God as suits you. But adopting deism is akin to putting your hands over your eyes and claiming the sun didn't come up.

Engage with God. Because He is, He is noticeable. He wants to be discovered and embraced.

But often on His terms, not yours.

Questions for Consideration

1. Where have you encountered deism?

2. Regarding the young man who died of cancer: Why would he adopt deism and what additional thought, or clarification, or piece of information might have protected him from deism during his days of suffering and trial?

3. What's your take on why Pascal could not forgive Descartes? Why was Descartes' belief such an affront to Pascal?

CHAPTER 15

JESUS CHRIST

I'm a writer.

There. I've made my claim. What are you going to do with this declaration of mine?

You'll search my name, and guess what? There I'll be. My books will be listed. You can buy them. You will conclude: He's who he says he is: a writer.

We judge people based upon what they declare about themselves. If you say you are from Cincinnati, you either are or you are not. If I ask, "How'd you like growing up in Tulsa?" you'll look at me funny.

Think about Jesus Christ a moment: He claimed to be God—which means, either He is or He is not.

Often, when people think about Jesus, they describe Him as a great, moral teacher. This is how Jews view Jesus, for example. Islam identifies Him as a prophet. Buddhists believe Jesus was enlightened and Hindus that He was *a* god (not *the* God), i.e. one god among their several million gods.

The problem is, Jesus didn't claim to be a moral teacher, a prophet, an enlightened person, or a god among the millions within Hinduism. Jesus Christ claimed to *be* God, *the* God. Evaluating Him, or classifying Him, as anything other than what He claimed is to misunderstand what He said about Himself.

When it comes to Jesus' claims about Himself, He didn't leave us much room for negotiation. Either He was God or He wasn't.

Prior to World War II, there was a famous atheist named C.S. Lewis who converted to Christianity. He's known for several books, like his fantasy series, *The Chronicles of Narnia*, but his most famous nonfiction work is *Mere Christianity*.

In *Mere Christianity* Lewis evaluates Jesus based upon what He claimed to be, i.e. the Son of God. Taking Him based upon His claim of divinity, Lewis concludes that Jesus' claim about Himself leaves only three options. The first option: Jesus was a liar. He claimed to be something He was not. The second option: He was a lunatic, a crazy man. After all, the only people who claim to be God are either in institutions or living under a bridge. Or third: He is exactly who He claimed to be: the God who is Lord of all.

Simple enough, isn't it? Yet, profound in implication.

As you start thinking about who Jesus was, let me offer three thoughts to get you started, one thought for each option Jesus' claim leaves you.

Was He a liar? History tells us two things about Jesus' followers, i.e. His disciples. First, all but one died a horrid death as a martyr. Only John died of natural causes, but he did so in exile on the Isle of Patmos. Here's the point to consider: Men die for something they believe. Second, the followers of Jesus never relinquished their story.

So, they died believing that Jesus was God, the long-awaited Messiah, and they died true to their belief. Perhaps one, maybe two, would die for a known or believed lie. But all of them? That's remarkable.

In 1972, there was a political scandal in the United States. In a quest to win reelection, President Nixon and his allies broke into the Democratic National Committee headquarters located in the Watergate Office Building in Washington, D.C. The perpetrators pledged loyalty and confidentiality… but once the scandal broke, the allegiances fell apart and the lies were inconsistent as each faced prison.

One of the President's men, Charles Colson, was convicted and sent to prison. While there, he read Lewis' *Mere Christianity.*

Mr. Colson knew firsthand that men don't die to preserve a lie. Within hours of being found out, he and his colleagues renounced their lie to try to save themselves. As he read about Jesus' disciples—all of them—going to death for their belief, and telling a consistent story, he determined the only explanation must be that Jesus was exactly who He claimed to be: the Son of God.

In prison, Chuck Colson gave his life to Jesus Christ because men don't die for something they know to be a lie.[72]

Was Jesus a lunatic? If so, then may the world have more lunatics born to us! Jesus brought mankind more love, compassion, hope, and care than any other human, societal system, or government in the history of the world.

Was He who He said: the Lord God?

If so, then it only makes sense to diligently figure out how His life and claims impact your life and eternal future. Anything less would be profound foolishness.[73]

---

72 You can read Charles Colson's story in his book, *Born Again*. A summary of what he thought of C.S. Lewis and the concept I'm referencing here in *Swagger* can be accessed at, "Chuck Colson on the Impact of CS Lewis' Mere Christianity," *The Poached Egg.net*. November 22, 2013. < https://www.thepoachedegg.net/2013/11/chuck-colson-on-the-impact-of-cs-lewis-mere-christianity.html>. Accessed, 17 July 2020.

73 To begin a relationship with Jesus Christ as God of your life, here are a few words—a prayer—to help you verbalize the intent of your heart and the decision you are making:

Jesus, I am convinced that you are who you claimed to be: God Incarnate, come to Earth, come to me. Thank you. First, I'm sorry it has taken so long for me to recognize who you are. I'm sorry for living independently of you. I'm sorry for the many ways in which I've offended you. Would you please forgive me? Second, I ask that you come into my life. Please take me into your family, secure my place in heaven when I die, and please live your powerful life through me for the remainder of my days. Thank you. Amen.

Toward the back of *Swagger* you will find a short chapter about becoming a Christian, i.e. a follower of Jesus Christ. It's titled, Appendix A. There is information about next steps as well as contact information. I look forward to helping you get started in your new way of living.

Questions for Consideration

1. A majority of people on Earth believe Jesus was a great teacher. On the one hand this is true, but why is this view shortsighted?

2. People do believe lies and die for them, e.g. Jim Jones' followers in Guyana.[74] What makes Jesus' disciples' actions—martyrdom and exile—different? Since Jonestown, how many more cult followers of Jones' have suicided? Since the death of Christ, how many Christian martyrs have there been? What's the value of this comparison?

3. Was Jesus a lunatic? What's your rationale?

---

74 Chiu, David. "Jonestown: 13 Things You Should Know About Cult Massacre." *RollingStone.com.* November 17, 2017. <https://www.rollingstone.com/culture/culture-features/jonestown-13-things-you-should-know-about-cult-massacre-121974/>. Accessed, 2 May 2020.

CHAPTER 16

LET'S ASSUME

I have an agnostic friend, Billy, and an atheist friend and neighbor, Tawny. The three of us were at Tawny's house having a drink together.

"Let me ask you a question," Billy said. "Let's assume—and this is a big assumption," he said with a nod to Tawny, "that there is a God."

"Well that's just stupid," interrupted Tawny.

"Let me finish," Billy persisted. "Preston, let's assume there is a God. Do you believe that He created everything, then backed away, and just took His hands off of His creation, or do you think God controls everything?"

"I don't believe either, Billy."

"Well, just assume one or the other."

"It's not one or the other—but if it were, I'd denounce God and be either an agnostic like you or an atheist like Tawny."

It was quiet for a moment while that probability settled in.

"Alright. So you don't believe either about God—assuming He exists?" Debating with Billy was like dancing with a Cobra. He was my friend, but one of the shrewdest people on the planet.

"No, I don't believe either. The idea that God created the world and took His hands off to let creation do as it pleased is called deism. Thomas Jefferson was a deist."

"That's good company," Billy said.

"Those people who believe that are by far the most rational among the religious," Tawny added.

"At the other end of your question is the idea that God controls everything. That's legalism, or what you term fundamentalism."

They began naming names of fundamentalists and people they felt should be categorized as such. It was a raucous naming and haphazard categorization, but I always appreciated hearing their views and perceptions. Hanging out with them was an education.

I continued. "Both of these views of God violate the most basic aspect of who He is portrayed to be in the Bible."

"How so?" asked Billy.

"Both remove the ability for man to meaningfully relate to God, one by a violation of his will—fundamentalism—and the other with an expansive distance that man cannot span. God did not create man for the heck of it, nor does He control man out of insecurity. He created to connect and relate."

"Oh, give me a footnote," cried Tawny. "This is conjecture, just a religious abstraction. Gee," he huffed. "Religion makes people crazy."

"You're not going to like my answer, Tawny."

"Well, go ahead. Try me."

"God realized He was abstract, unknowable. To quote you, He knew He needed to 'descend the abstraction' and make Himself approachable. That's why He incarnated Himself in the person of Jesus Christ."

Tawny went to refresh his drink.

Billy said, "I see what you're saying. I don't agree, but I understand."

"Billy, here's the deal: Assuming God exists, and He is the God I just described, then He has to be big enough and secure enough for a man to ask Him to prove Himself to him."

"Yes, that's correct. He'd have to be absolutely secure enough for that."

Questions for Consideration

1. What's wrong with God creating the universe, then retiring? What's wrong with God controlling everything?

2. Why do you guess Tawny felt religion makes people crazy?

3. What's your understanding of the Incarnation and the rationale behind it?

CHAPTER 17

WHY IS CHRISTIANITY UNIQUE?

Of all the religions in the world, and all the gods in the universe, Christianity is unique in this: The God of Christianity comes to you instead of requiring that you get to Him or find Him.

Every other religion requires that you do something to find their god. Assuming you find that god, there is a long list of things to do in order to please that god and keep him, or her, or it happy.

The God of Christianity understands that you do not have a chance of earning His acceptance through your own efforts. His standard is perfection. So, He makes a way for you to be accepted unconditionally by Him through Jesus Christ—who was God, but took on human flesh and came to us so that He could understand all our pressures, feel our concerns, suffer as we do, take our failures upon Himself, and in so doing, provide a way to God.

The good news that Christianity teaches is that God came to us in the man called Jesus Christ. In Jesus Christ, God comes to us, searches us out, finds us, engages us, courts us, and invites us into His forever family. When Christmas comes around next, this is what the holiday is celebrating: God Incarnate, i.e. Jesus Christ.

When someone talks about all religions being equal, you'll know better.

When someone gives an inspirational talk about finding God, you'll know better—about who finds who when it comes to the God of Christianity.

Christianity is exclusive, just as its critics assert. But it's exclusive because of what its God *does* versus what every other god *requires*.

Questions for Consideration

1. Consider the first two paragraphs. Think through what you know of other religions. Is the claim made in the opening paragraphs valid?

2. Is there really nothing you can do to enhance your standing with God? Why?

3. Why does it matter whether or not Christianity is unique among the world's religions?

CHAPTER 18

CAN CHRISTIANITY BE PROVEN?

People describe coming to faith in Jesus Christ as a leap of faith—like jumping across a chasm so wide that it is impossible to cross without the bridge of faith.

I understand the point, i.e. to underscore the importance of faith and the impossibility of gaining acceptance with God by anything other than faith, but I argue against the chasm image because it implies that Christianity is irrational, mindless, and even foolish compared to logic and reason.

But can Christianity be proven?

If by "proven" we mean scientific proof, then no. Christianity can't be proven in the same way gravity is proven because Christianity is not a natural law. This doesn't mean it's not true—only that it is established by another means of proof than how scientists prove something, but equally valid.

At its heart, Christianity is a relationship and relationships are not proven, they are embraced consensually, and thus established. A relationship is a fact. It is observable. Relationships are numerous and similar, but each is unique. These qualities hint at proof, but they lack the control required of scientific proof.

A forced relationship, i.e. one without choice, is abusive, one-sided. A forced sexual relationship is called rape. A forced allegiance is called coercion. A tyrannical relationship has subjects, not citizens, and required relationship is called slavery.

The fact that Christianity requires faith—belief, free choice, willfulness— proves it is relational and respectful, not that it is irrational or unscientific. You may as well ask your dog to prove the quadratic equation as ask science to prove Christianity. Dogs don't do algebra and science doesn't do metaphysics.

Don't get me wrong though. Just because Christianity is entered into by faith doesn't mean it is irrational, unscientific, or mindless.

We could say the same things about marriage—another relationship—that we are saying about Christianity. Entering into a life-long commitment requires an element of faith and belief. It is also rational, proven, sobering, and replicable in general terms.

Proof doesn't tolerate doubt. In the scientific world, beliefs or theories are tested until proven, and once proven, doubt is removed. A scientific law is established.

But Christianity is no more a law than marriage is. You are free to participate or not. Whether entering into relationship with God via Christianity, or saying yes to a marriage proposal, both require faith and belief in the other person.

God won't force you to believe by leaving you no rational choice. That would be a forced relationship. God invites you to believe, to join Him, to enjoy life together, and forge a bond into eternity. While His invitation is compelling, it isn't compulsory. You are free to enter in or to opt out.

In this sense, Christianity is true, just like marriage is true. But you can't prove Christianity any more than you can prove love.

But when you get married, it is not a blind leap into a dark chasm. You look carefully before you say, "I do." The same is true of Christianity. It's not a blind leap of faith any more than marriage is.

God wouldn't ask that of you. He's far too reasonable for that.

So, can Christianity be proven?

What this question is really asking is, can I truly have a viable relationship with God?

The answer to the question is, absolutely. It's a fact.

God made provision through Jesus Christ for you to relate to Him, because when everything is said and done, God truly desires to have a viable relationship with you.

Questions for Consideration

1. Is Christian belief inferior to logic and reason? Why or why not?

2. If Christianity is intended to be relational—God and man in relationship—then why is belief important? If all you do is believe, is that good enough to be a Christian?

3. What is the risk of not believing? What is the benefit of believing?

CHAPTER 19

WHAT IS A CHRISTIAN?

A Christian is a person who has pledged their life and future to God based upon their belief in Jesus Christ to forgive their sins and transform them into a new, spiritual person. They believe Jesus Christ lives in them through the presence of the Holy Spirit of God. As a result, a Christian believes they will live eternally in heaven with God.

A Christian is not affiliated with a political party. Nor is a Christian someone who attends a particular church. The Bible says a Christian is recognized by the way they love others.[75]

Sadly, at the time of this writing, Christianity has been politicized and is considered a voting block large enough that political candidates court

---

75 John 13:35. NASB.

"Christian" votes. Currently, this is a conservative voting block described as "far right" and "fundamentalist." Besides simplistic, such designations are flat wrong, just as categorical declarations of any other group are simplistic and wrong.

True Christianity is not a socio-political block. In fact, the Book of Acts in the Bible says that followers of Jesus Christ, i.e. His disciples, were first called Christians in a city called Antioch.[76, 77]

As of this writing, many Christians are using synonymous terms for Christianity to describe themselves, e.g. a follower of Jesus Christ, a Christ-follower, a Believer. This is because the term "Christian" has been so politicized. The same is true for the term "evangelical."

A person devoted to Jesus Christ—a Christian—is not looking to Christianity to make them comfortable. They certainly enjoy the fact their sins are forgiven and their eternal destiny is secure in heaven, but they realize Christianity is not about comfort. Christianity is about transformation. It is about spiritual growth.

A Christian is a person whose life is changed—and experientially changing—from self-rule to Christ-run. Not for a little while, but from now on.

---

76 Acts 11:26. NASB.

77 Encyclopedia Britannica. "Antioch: Modern and Ancient City, South-Central Turkey." *Britannica.com*. <https://www.britannica.com/place/Antioch-modern-and-ancient-city-south-central-Turkey>. Ancient Antioch is the modern city of Antakya, Turkey. It is situated near the mouth of the Orontes River, northwest of the Syrian border. It was an early center of Christianity.

A Christian believes God is gracious to accept their appeal for new life, forgive their independence and the fallacies of their independent ways, i.e. what the Bible calls sin, and make them part of His family. A Christian believes that God gives them a new identity as His child, and then sets about introducing and integrating them into the ways of His family, while conforming their behavior to match that of Jesus Christ.

Christianity has answers to many of life's pressing questions. However, Christians understand—or should realize—that their faith in Christ, and their confidence in the Bible as divinely inspired, does not render a categorical, formulaic faith. Christianity speaks to many issues, but it is not an exhaustive encyclopedia of all the correct answers to life's conundrums.

More than anything, Christians enjoy relationship with God who engages their life, present and future. They believe God's pledge to never leave them nor forsake them.[78]

A Christian is a person who knows they had an option to pursue life either on their own or in concert with God. They chose the latter, and in so doing, joined God's life in them and through them.

Note: If you are not a follower of Jesus Christ, i.e. a Christian, and would like to be, turn to Appendix A for more information.

---

78 Cf.: Hebrews 13:5, et al. NASB.

Questions for Consideration

1. What is your opinion of Christianity and Christians? How was your belief formed?

2. Christianity is about transformation. It is about spiritual growth. It is not a religion you adopt to find comfort and happiness. Agree or disagree—and why?

3. Christianity involves recognizing and declaring God to be supreme in your life, Lord of all you are and do, King of you. How do you feel about this? Is there a workaround to avoid this? What might that look like?

CHAPTER 20

BLAME

In the June 24, 2019 issue of *The Atlantic*, author Lyman Stone's opening sentence states, "The Baby Boomers ruined America."[79]

I'm a Baby Boomer (1946-1964), born in 1956. All the problems you face as a human being are the fault of my generation according to Mr. Stone. So, if you've been wondering who to blame, apparently I'm your guy.

Since this criticism is specifically about what Boomers have done to America, I'm going to write my next words as an American, from an American perspective. However, if you are reading these lines and live outside the United States of America, my words still apply. As they say, there's enough blame to go around.

---

79 Stone, Lyman. "The Boomers Ruined Everything." *TheAtlantic.com*. June 24, 2019. https://www. theatlantic.com/ideas/archive/2019/06/boomers-are-blame-aging-america/592336/>. Accessed, 24 April 2020.

Mr. Stone's list of grievances is long. He begins by noting that political institutions are frozen in time. The average state constitution is more than 100 years old and America is in its third-longest period without a constitutional amendment.

He continues, citing these issues: Lower cuts to retiree benefits. Student debt, climate change, and low birth rates are ignored. Institutions are less dynamic. Housing, work rules, higher education, law enforcement, public budgeting—all suffer from stricter regulation.

Author Stone summarizes: "Boomers have created a crisis for younger Americans."

Then he resumes the list of wrongs: Zoning codes are rooted in the 1900s. There are outdated terms in Google's database of American English. Increased land-use rules, e.g. rules about parking, green space, building height limits, neighborhood aesthetics, historic preservation, and new construction—all making Boomers responsible for creating lifestyle difficulties for everyone else in America, which limits their childbearing and entry into adulthood, he asserts.

Having trouble getting pregnant? Stuck in adolescence? Now you know why.

Continuing: Boomers made rules to keep young people from buying homes, finding employment, and increased the requirements for licenses, degrees, and certificates. We made university education not as financially profitable as it once was. Incarceration rates have increased, as have student debt, credit card loans, entitlements, pensions, Social Security and Medicare costs, federal and state debt. All of this inevitably must increase taxes. Also the fault of the Baby Boomers: streets with more potholes, worse schools, and higher death rates for 32-year-olds, i.e. those who are of prime working age.

After creating all this ruination, Mr. Stone laments that "Baby Boomers are living longer even as the workers who pay for their pensions are dying from an epidemic of drug overdose, suicide, car accidents, and violence." Oh yes, and because Boomers live longer, the cost of health care is increasing.

How thoughtless could a group of people be? Die already.

Is *The Atlantic* article extreme?

It's in print. Magazines don't generally print stuff their readers won't read or don't embrace. And for the record, Mr. Stone's is not a lone voice. Larry Getlen reviewed Jill Filipovic's new book for the *New York Post*. Based upon the excerpts he quotes, Ms. Filipovic sounds a similar refrain to Mr. Stone's tune. While noting that the oldest Millennials are now 40 years old, Filipovic writes. "We're only now starting to grasp the degree to which we have gotten screwed."[80]

Blame is powerful. It absolves the one blaming of responsibility.

One thing is certain: If I'm ever in the room with Mr. Stone, I will not turn my back to him.

---

80 Getlen, Larry. "Why Millennials' Distaste for Baby Boomers is Justified." *NYPost.com*. August 8, 2020. <https://nypost.com/2020/08/08/why-millennials-distaste-for-baby-boomers-is-justified/>. Accessed, August 14, 2020.

But, what is Mr. Stone's point?

I think what author Stone is saying is that he is unhappy and it's someone else's fault.

Blame has its place. Absolute blame is always a signal that something is amiss.

That Mr. Stone places responsibility for his happiness in the hands of someone else says something bad about Mr. Stone, not the people he believes should make him happy.

Mr. Stone might be wise to read the work of Viktor Frankel, a Jew imprisoned in a death camp by the Nazis during their Holocaust. Naked, alone, his life's work destroyed, Frankel concluded there was one thing no one could take away: his freedom of choice.

Happiness is not bequeathed to you nor is it something you find. Happiness is a choice you make.

Life is demanding. Life is a hard job. There is no warranty. *Caveat emptor* (let the buyer beware).

From my reading of Mr. Stone, I believe there are three options: 1) Whine, like Lyman Stone. 2) Embrace ingenuity and determination. 3) Liquidate the old people and old things.

At times passively by implication, at times actively, Author Stone is advocating for option 3: elimination of all that is old, both people and systems. His opinion has wide acceptance across all sectors of society.

As you might guess, I disagree with both the figurative and literal execution of option 3—and not just because I'm a Boomer. Elimination is absolute. It requires starting all over. Historically this is called a revolution and those tend to be brutal, bloody, and regressive.

Blame is enticing. It's linked to justification: I'm right, you're wrong. The problem with justification is, a) no one is left standing except you, and b) very few things in life are right and wrong. Life is a nuanced endeavor that you slice and dice, not a categorical choice that responds well to being hammered upon.

Blame is binary: yes or no, either or. Actually, life is analog and multi-faceted.

Blame is enticing because it's also linked to revenge. Who doesn't like to see the bully get his comeuppance?

The problem with revenge is that you are incapable of doing it well, i.e. to the extent it needs to be done. The Bible says, "Do not take revenge yourselves, dear friends, but give place to God's wrath, for it is written, 'Vengeance is mine, I will repay,' says the Lord."[81]

I understand wanting revenge and exacting vengeance. I've tried it. Here's the deal: Vengeance is so profound, so heavy, so important that we don't stand a chance of doing it correctly or getting it right. If we try, it will break us. If you haven't yet met someone eaten up with bitterness, you will. It's sobering.

---

81 Romans 12:19. Holy Bible. *Lexham English Bible* (LEB). Logos Bible Software. 2012.

I heard the late Kenny Rogers say, "Revenge is like eating a cold supper." He was loosely quoting his character in *Rio Diablo*, Quentin Leech.[82]

Eliminating all that is old is either incredible genius or incredible ignorance. Both are arrogant, and either way, the risk is significant that not all will buy in. That's why such ideas are called revolutions.

Since blame is rarely categorical, there is merit in considering who draws the lines of fault where.

Elimination of old people (geronticide or euthanasia) and ideas (revolution) is a dangerous path to adopt because it places arbitrary value on human life and endeavor. Who decides who no longer gets to live? Who decides a person or an idea is wrong because they are old—and how old is too old?

If Mr. Stone was in charge, all states in America whose constitutions are 100 years old or older would be tossed and new constitutions drafted. Those state's constitutions are wrong, not because of what they say, but because they are a century old. The Constitution would be amended—with something to be determined—simply because it's overdue for a correction.

It is legal (as of this writing) to terminate the most innocent among us: babies *in utero* (i.e., in the uterus or womb). As a society, we argue strongly that this is a fundamental right. What becomes of us—actually, what becomes of you since I'll be dead—if you also terminate the most vulnerable: old people?

---

82 Hardy, Rod, Director. *Rio Diablo*. 1992. *DigitallyObsessed.com*. <http://www.digitallyobsessed.com/displaylegacy.php?ID=4985>. Accessed, 16 July 2020.

And if you get sick with some dread ill, or are afflicted with diabetes, or are broken up and crippled in a tragedy, what will keep a mercenary society from concluding your life because you are no longer seen as useful, or are a drain, or can no longer contribute, or...?

Or what if society arbitrarily decides your ideas, or your politics, or your religion, or your place of origin, or your financial status are to blame for society's ills, unhappiness, financial debt...?

You presume this would never happen. Surely your generation would be more principled than to be punitive or capricious. Surely your generation would figure out an equitable solution.

Yes, surely. But blame is enticing. The alternative is personal responsibility for difficult issues.

As I write this chapter to you, vast swaths of the civilized world eliminate their undesirables: infirmed, dissidents, females, criminals, the elderly, orphans, those of other races, those *in utero*. Humanity has killed multitudes more who are inconvenient or undesirable than all the wars have killed in the long history of the world. If you add the figurative killing of souls through imprisonment, torture, poverty, discrimination, tyranny, and abuse the number of those taken out from among us numbers in the many billions.

I'm arguing for the value of human life, i.e. literal life as well as figurative life that we produce through our ideas and perspectives. Valuing life is a constant struggle for our species.

Blame is powerful denial and the appeal of that elusive happiness is intoxicating enough to sacrifice another to possess it.

Option 1 remains an option. You can whine. Be forewarned though: Your soul will wither and become timid.

President Theodore Roosevelt said, "It is not the critic who counts; not the man who points out how the strong man stumbles, or where the doer of deeds could have done them better. The credit belongs to the man who is actually in the arena, whose face is marred by dust and sweat and blood; who strives valiantly; who errs, who comes short again and again, because there is no effort without error and shortcoming; but who does actually strive to do the deeds; who knows great enthusiasms, the great devotions; who spends himself in a worthy cause; who at the best knows in the end the triumph of high achievement, and who at the worst, if he fails, at least fails while daring greatly, so that his place shall never be with those cold and timid souls who neither know victory nor defeat."[83]

The floor of every arena—society, marriage, friendship, university, profession, business—is dirty. You have three choices: 1) whine and never get in the arena, 2) step into the arena, or 3) project blame onto those in the arena.

In place of blame, option 2 is compelling. It is responsible, realistic, determined, and gracious. It manages just blame by drawing upon its critique for guidance while simultaneously unleashing the indomitable human spirit, i.e. personal responsibility.

---

83 McCarthy, Erin. "Roosevelt's 'The Man in the Arena.'" *MentalFloss.com*. April 23, 2015 and 2020. <https://www.mentalfloss.com/article/63389/roosevelts-man-arena>. Accessed, 24 April 2020.

"Through every generation of the human race there has been a constant war, a war with fear. Those who have the courage to conquer it are made free and those who are conquered by it are made to suffer until they have the courage to defeat it, or death takes them." Those are the words of Alexander the Great.[84]

Life is a wild, dangerous, wonderful, and ultimately terminal proposition. It can be scary. It can be exhilarating. It's your choice how you meet the day.

You can whine, and Mr. Stone sets a good example of how to do this.

You can eliminate all that doesn't suit you. But I should warn you: Established ideas have weathered time for a reason and seasoned travelers through humanity's journey didn't get to be old by being timid.

You can step into the arena and seize life by the horns.

---

84 Alexander the Great. *Goodreads.com.* <https://www.goodreads.com/quotes/7912421-through-every-generation-of-the-human-race-there-has-been>. Accessed, 24 April 2020.

Questions for Consideration

1. Mr. Stone cites conditions that in his thinking prove that Baby Boomers have ruined America for subsequent generations. How do you feel about what he's saying?

2. What circumstances would need to exist for western civilization to adopt a standard defining an acceptable quality of life, and as long as a person passes these standards, e.g. productive contributor to business, part of the tax base, good physical health, etc., then they are legitimate, but if they fall below the standards, e.g. old, infirmed, mentally deficient, then they are medically terminated for the overall good of society?

3. Are there times and circumstances when blame is legitimate, warranted, and okay?

CHAPTER 21

SHAME

I don't remember when Mom first asked as I was headed out the door, "Do you have on clean underwear?"

Eventually this became a Gillham-family joke, but early on, I knew Mom was serious. If something happened to me while I was out, and I ended up at the hospital or the morgue, Mom wanted to know she would not be ashamed that I had on dirty underwear. Later, the joke was that wearing clean underwear was more important than our well-being, but that was only later.

Shame is powerful. If appearance and performance are the currencies that earn acceptance and approval, then an unkempt appearance or poor performance are shameful.

Around 370 years before Christ was born, Plato penned a work titled, *Phaedrus*. It's an imaginary discussion between his mentor, Socrates, and a young man named, Phaedrus. In the discussion, Socrates illustrates the concept of right as being like a magnificent horse that has no need of the whip, "…but is guided by word and admonition only," and is always obedient because of "…the government of shame."[85]

Socrates is saying, through the authorship of Plato, that what is right isn't done by humankind because it is the right thing to do, but for fear of being shamed and ashamed. Even given its honor and nobility, right is too weak to reliably govern itself. A stronger force is necessary to supply sufficient incentive if right is to prevail, for appearance to be maintained, and performance to be exemplary. No resolution of willpower is strong enough. Only the perpetual government of shame can reliably deliver what is right.

Mom battled perfectionism. This isn't a family secret. She spoke about it and wrote about it often. For much of my life, she lost that battle regularly, requiring perfection of herself and me. When I failed, the shame lasted for days—both in her and in me.

As I got older, I realized that perfection was unreasonable. In fact, when I did something perfectly, it often still didn't meet the standard. I couldn't buck Mom, or confront her, or reason with her. Well, I guess I could have, but now we are back to the matter of showing up at the morgue with clean underwear.

---

85 Plato. *Phaedrus*. Translated by Benjamin Jowett. Public Domain. P. 18.

My eventual plan for survival was to figure out what the right thing was to do, then do my best to perform what was right. While perfection was unreasonable, doing the right thing was reasonable. Like Hunter Thompson, "Anything worth doing, is worth doing right."[86]

Doing the right thing enabled me to manage Mom within my own head. If right wasn't good enough, and she got wormy over the lack of perfection, I endured her attempt to shame me with the comfort that I did what was right to the best of my ability.

I never told Mother this. I simply nodded when she placed shame upon me, as though I was taking her shame upon myself, then jettisoned it as soon as possible and assuaged my offended soul with the reassurance that I had done what was right.

Navigating Mom's (and Dad's) governance empowered by shame served me okay while I was at home. But shame ambushed me. While I knew Mom fought this dragon, I didn't realize I adopted a similar method for managing my own appearance and performance.

In both Mom's and my economy, acceptance was not granted, it was earned. For Mom, perfect performance and appearance rendered acceptance. For me, doing the right thing, and looking right while doing it, rendered acceptance.

---

86 Thompson, Hunter S. *GoodReads.com*. <https://www.goodreads.com/quotes/76425-anything-worth-doing-is-worth-doing-right>. Accessed, 30 April 2020.

For both of us, others were easily managed through our intentional appearance and performance. The hardest person for Mom to please was herself, because she knew better. For me, the most ruthless person on the planet when I failed to do the right thing was me—in truth, *is* me.

Mom was a wildly talented, articulate, beautiful, and winsome woman (she's gone now, but you can read about her on my website[87]). She could outperform nearly anyone on the planet with one arm tied behind her back.

Mom fought—she's now free of her delusional philosophy—to attain self-acceptance. When Mom failed, she got depressed.

When I fail, I'm brutal—to me.

The governance of shame is meted out in ruthless self-criticism, condemnation, ranting, raving, self-cursing, and condescension. The government of shame is dismissive, demeaning, discounting, derisive, and abusive. If right appearance and performance produce acceptance, then no mercy can be shown for any compromise of self-rightness.

It doesn't matter who you read: Plato, Freud, Glasser, Maslow, Fromm, Frankel, Lewis, the Old Testament, or the New Testament—they all agree: If you as a human being are insecure about your love and acceptance, you are afflicted with a major impediment. All forces within reach of your soul will be brought to bear until unconditional love and acceptance are secured.

---

87 Gillham, Preston. "Anabel." *PrestonGillham.com*. <http://www.prestongillham.com/blog/anabel>. Accessed, 30 April 2020.

This is the simple logic behind God telling us that He is love.[88] For all of what must be an infinite list of character qualities, God reduces His identifying marker to one thing: love. Period. God is saying, "While there's a lot more to know about me, that's all you *need* to know."

What's powerful about shame is its declaration that unconditional love and acceptance don't exist. One of the most famous people to diligently read Plato was Augustine who lived six hundred years later and wrote a book titled, *Confessions*. As a young man, Augustine tried everything there was in the world to try. He committed sins I've never heard of. But upon his wicked journey of life, Augustine gave his life to Jesus Christ, and as He always does, Jesus turned debauched Augustine into the man we know as St. Augustine.

The transformation was astounding, as you can read in his book—and, his influence was remarkable. Out of his theological thinking—the man was brilliant—came what we know as Catholicism. Of course, Catholic theology is a compendium of thoughts collected over 2500 years, but Augustine's devotion to confession significantly influenced how Catholic theology believes God manages mankind.

Backing up a step, Augustine and Plato were somewhat kindred souls even though separated by six centuries. Both longed to overcome his moral, ethical, and human failings. Both tried to manage his dark side with the power entrusted to a government of shame.

---

88 1 John 4:8. NASB.

Thomas Cahill describes how Augustine studied Plato, desperately wanting—needing—something more, but failing to find it in Plato's writings. "Who else even talks of these things," he wondered. "And then the answer comes to him: Saul of Tarsus, the wiry, bald-headed Jew whose awkward, importunate letters, signed 'Paul,' the Christians have been using as scripture."[89]

Augustine read St. Paul. He returned to Plato's writings. He needed relief from his guilt.

Plato advanced—in all fairness, three centuries before Christ came—that to ascend to God, man must attain to truth and right, and live by wisdom. The incentive to do this is shame. Negatively stated, management of failure is through a government of shame.

But in Paul's writing, Augustine realized that he would never realize his goal of true living via governance by shame. It was disheartening. If the government of shame could not fix his addiction to debauchery, as powerful as shame is, and if Paul was correct in saying that only intervention by God could produce change, then what hope was there for true change in a life so fouled up and so distant from God?

Considering all his wrongs and misery, Augustine writes, "From a hidden depth a profound self-examination had dredged up a heap of all my misery and set it 'in the sight of my heart' (Psalm 18:15). That precipitated a vast storm bearing a massive downpour of tears."[90]

---

89 Cahill, Thomas. *How the Irish Saved Civilization*. Anchor Books. New York, NY. 1995. P. 56.

90 Augustine. *Confessions*. Translated by Henry Chadwick. Oxford University Press. 1991. P. 152.

He continued to study St. Paul's writings. Eventually, Augustine submits himself to God, becomes a disciple of Jesus Christ, and is baptized. The change in Augustine is profound.

Paul's discussion about the battle between flesh and spirit[91] gives him the hope he has needed. But it seems from reading his *Confessions* that he missed Paul's message about forgiveness and acceptance in Christ.

While all of us who call upon the name of Christ are saved into a new life and transformed, none of us achieve perfect clarity about what this truly means. For Augustine, he clung to Plato's governance by shame even while calling upon the Holy Spirit of God to help him overcome the lusts of his flesh.

This theology is still pervasive in Catholic belief today. It is not grace-based, but shame-based, with attending punishments until penance is served. I'm not a Catholic, but I relate.

As powerful as shame is, and as potent as self-condemnation is, these are insufficient to create in us lasting change or gain for us the unconditional love and acceptance that is essential. When Saul of Tarsus, the wiry, bald-headed Jew that Cahill references, was confronted by Jesus Christ on the road to Damascus and was converted,[92] not only was his name changed to Paul, he was changed, transformed, and set upon a fresh course.

---

91 Cf.: Galatians 5:16. NASB.

92 Acts 9:1-19. NASB.

Paul was highly educated in all things Jewish and all things Greek. When he gives his sermon in Athens, he quotes a couple of obscure Greek thinkers.[93] This, along with a linguistic look at Paul's writing, indicate he knew the work of Plato. But, Paul disagreed with Plato. More accurately, based upon the finished work of Jesus Christ, Paul understood that God had provided a means by which the battle between flesh and spirit could be won, thus doing for us through Christ what the government of shame is incapable of achieving.

It's an amazing theology that Plato didn't know—couldn't know—since Christ had not come yet. It is a theology Augustine couldn't quite bring fully aboard such that the guilt of his debauchery prior to salvation was washed clean through Christ's forgiveness.

One of these days, I'll know for certain, but for now I'm left to project my speculation upon Augustine. I'm guessing that if backed into an intellectual and theological corner, he would say God had forgiven him all his sins and sinfulness through Jesus Christ, but the intensity of his continuing struggle rendered his practical battling of flesh against spirit a conflict governed by shame. Thus, the belief that his ongoing confessions are necessary for acceptance with God. His book is appropriately titled.

For Paul, unconditional love and acceptance by God are established and guaranteed by Jesus Christ. Nothing that he does can diminish these, nothing he does can enhance these.

---

93 Cf.: Acts 17:22-31. NASB.

Our greatest need, our most-essential need following food and shelter, is met by God in Christ.[94] That the battle between flesh and spirit continues to rage in this earthly life is another subject[95] and has no bearing on whether or not we are unconditionally loved and accepted by God through the finished work of Jesus Christ.

Plato sensed this. Augustine sought this. Paul knew this. He wrote it down for us.[96] He struggled to bring what he knew to render consistent victory in his battle against the flesh, but he knew that God indeed intervened fully in Jesus Christ. He intervened fully in that His intervention leaves no role nor need for shame.

Mom knew what Paul knew. She wrote books about victory over the flesh. She told stories about knowing she was loved and accepted by God. She smiled when my brothers and I joked about having on clean underwear as we headed out the door, but I don't recall her ever outright denying that it was no longer important to her sense of standing as a mom who did a good job—should she be evaluated by an ER doc or the mortician. What I do know is that she battled her despondency in real terms and actual days. She knew what Paul knew, but like him, she could also have penned a confession like Paul's in Romans 7.

---

94 Cf.: Philippians 4:19. NASB.

95 To read more about the conflict between flesh and spirit in the form of a novel and adventure story: Gillham, Preston. *No Mercy.* Bonefish Publication. Fort Worth, TX. 2010.

96 Romans 7:7-25. NASB.

And, I know what Paul wrote and what Jesus Christ accomplished on my behalf in terms of acceptance and love. I too have written books on the subject.[97] I've lectured on this all over the world. I write about it still in the articles I pen.[98]

But.

But, like Augustine and Socrates in Plato's *Phaedrus*, governance through shame is mighty tempting. In fact, if I fail to do what is right—especially if I should have known better—it is almost like I default to a government of shame, never pausing to consider the grace that is mine as a child of God.

That's the bad report from me to you. That's my confession, to use Augustine's language.

The good news is that after I've gone on a self-indicting, self-cursing, self-condemning rant and all the world around me goes quiet under the weight of shame, I realize I've adopted a governance model that is insufficient for what my soul truly needs.

For shame to work most powerfully, it must marinate. But in Christ there is grace and forgiveness for the moment, even a shameful moment. No matter how profoundly my wrong decisions lead me off into the swamp, God has already intervened with all I need to live a forgiven life. There is nothing for shame to contribute. Secondly, no matter the morass I wander into, there is

---

97 Cf.: *No Mercy* and *Battle for the Round Tower*. Bonefish Publication. Fort Worth, TX. 2010, 2013.

98 Cf.: *PrestonGillham.com/blog*.

nothing that can separate me from the love and acceptance of God. There is no need to call upon shame to find my way back to God. He is already present.[99]

Still, when I fail—and I do with discouraging frequency—I know what to do.

I back up to the point in my memory where I switched from the acceptance and love that are mine because of Jesus Christ and adopted the government of shame to see me through. Once identified, at that mental point where I made the wrong choice, I say, "Father God, it's at that point I embraced the belief that shame could deliver to me the most important things in life. I apologize to you, and I apologize to me.

"I see where I went wrong. Would you please guide me in learning from this mistake, this sin of shame, so that when this temptation occurs again, I will see more clearly? I realize I have failed to perform right and I deeply desire for my performance and appearance to match what is true of me.

"Speaking of which, thank you that nothing I do, or fail to do, will ever alter the acceptance and love I have in you."

Then, wherever I am, in whatever state, disposition, or outlook, I envision locking arms with God, Jesus, and the Holy Spirit to guide me toward my true heart's desire.

This is the alternative to a government of shame.

---

99 Cf.: Romans 8:37-39. NASB.

And just in case you are wondering, the answer is, yes. Mom's worries over my underwear were persistent enough, long enough, with enough repletion that clean undies are my priority as well. In fact, I have twelve pairs: January, February, March....

Questions for Consideration

1. Whose philosophy makes the most sense to you, and whose do you believe most helpful: Plato's or Paul's? What leads you to your belief?

2. Does unconditional acceptance truly exist, i.e. it's not just a concept? If so, what can you do to secure it, enhance it, or diminish it?

3. If you are totally and unconditionally accepted by God—or anyone else—are you free to live and do as you please knowing your acceptance is secure? If yes, why? If no, what constrains you?

Chapter 22

QUITTING

Up in the mountains above Los Angeles, near San Bernardino, there is a resort called Arrowhead Springs.[100] It used to be the hangout for movie stars, and then became the headquarters of Campus Crusade for Christ before they relocated to Orlando. I was there, invited to speak to a select group of Crusade staff, and was assigned a driver by the name of Carl to transport me from my bungalow, through the sprawling property, to headquarters for my meetings.

In addition to campus ministries, Crusade also had a redemptive program for ex-convicts—a half-way house concept—hoping that by providing life skills and spiritual teaching they would have a better chance of successfully

---

100 Nolan, Ruth. "The Arrow Rises Again: San Bernardino's Famed and Forgotten Architectural Wonder." *KCET.org*. May 2, 2017. <https://www.kcet.org/shows/artbound/the-arrow-rises-again-san-bernardinos-famed-and-forgotten-architectural-wonder>. Accessed, 24 April 2020.

reentering society after years in prison. Carl was an ex-con and couldn't have fit the stereotype of a man who'd done hard time any better if he'd been cast by Hollywood. He had a hard, lean demeanor. His mouth twitched with nervous energy and his hair was slicked back with enough grease to cause an ecological disaster should he go into the ocean.

Each morning as I opened the door of my bungalow, Carl sat waiting, crouched low in the driver's seat of a brown Oldsmobile station wagon whose springs and shocks had long since given up their duties. I would speak, Carl would nod. Then, creeping out the drive and up the hill, he drove me to headquarters. It did not escape me that I could have walked faster, but I was Carl's responsibility and in his care.

In each session, a few moments after I began lecturing, Carl slipped into the back of the room, warily looked left and right, and once satisfied he was unnoticed, leaned against the back wall, one foot bent under him against the wall, arms crossed in a surly dare. I eyed him as I taught, glad he was on my team, assuming he was on my team, hoping this was the case. I couldn't get a good read on Carl.

After my third lecture, Carl began asking questions—short, pointed, incisive—shrewder questions than any regular attendee was posing. I answered, wondering if a conversation would ensue. With his right wrist draped over the Oldsmobile's steering wheel, Carl simply nodded once as he took my reply aboard, and drove steadily onward.

On the way to headquarters one evening, Carl said, "I told my roommates about your talks."

"Oh, that right?"

Carl nodded. Once. Creeping up the hill toward headquarters.

"They'd like to talk to you. Asked me to see if you'd come up after you're done talking."

"Sure. Of course. I'd be happy to do that."

Carl was waiting in the Oldsmobile under the *porte cochère* when I exited the headquarters lobby. His eyes were squinted. Hard. He was grinding his teeth, his jaw muscle's walnut-sized knots flexing through his cheek-skin. No nod. Stared, waiting for me to fasten my seatbelt, then idled away, down toward the front gate. Carl was on a drop mission. I was the goods.

When we exited Arrowhead Springs, Carl turned up the mountain, away from the lights. Steadily, slowly, creeping up into the San Bernardino mountains on a winding road. The lights disappeared. The dash lights glowing on his etched face, Carl didn't say a word.

I have no idea how the builder built the house where Carl and his roommates lived. It hung precariously on a cliff that in the dark appeared to hover above an abyss. Looking west, the lights of the L.A. basin twinkled, dozens of miles in the distance.

Gravel crunched in the drive as Carl turned off the blacktop. He eased to a stop, shut off the Oldsmobile, got out, and stood by the fender.

A hulking man waited at the front door, backlit. There were no words, sparse movement. I stepped toward the front door. "Hi, I'm Preston."

The big man nodded once. "Billy. Thanks for coming." He held the door and moved aside.

Three other men stood in the yellow-lit room, their hands clasped in front of them. Each nodded, none spoke. Billy and Carl joined them, forming a semi-circle before me.

Billy said, "Well, you already know Carl here. I told you I'm Billy. Been in San Quentin, Folsom, Avenal. Assault, armed robbery...." He mulled over his other sins against society—the additional crimes he could confess, but two were enough he decided. Glancing left, "This one here's Tom." Tom stepped forward, offered me his hand, nodded, and stepped back. "He's out of Alcatraz, one of the last before they closed it. Then Lompoc." Billy shrugged. "Robbery, manslaughter—voluntary."

Billy introduced the other two, Johnny and Mike, and just like Tom, when he said their name, they stepped forward, shook my hand, and stepped back as Billy recited the short-list of their convictions. I'd never heard of several prisons Billy named, but I'd heard of all the crimes committed and figured each lock-up dealt out hard time as brutally as the prisons made famous by Johnny Cash's songs: San Quentin and Folsom.

Introductions done, Billy motioned Carl forward with his head. Carl pointed me toward the middle cushion of a lime-green sofa covered in plastic, "You'll sit here."

When I moved, the others moved, collected the kitchen chairs and an orphaned cane-back, arranged them in a semi-circle before me, and sat down. No crossed legs. Feet flat on the floor.

Billy leaned forward, studying me, casing me, considering the measure of me. "Carl says he thinks you can help us."

I didn't know why I was brought up the mountain, but helping five ex-convicts with something they were planning hadn't crossed my mind. I pursed my lips, tilted my head, "Okay, what's going on?" as I thought, *I don't know anything about robbing banks or shooting people—and I sure don't want any part of San Quentin.*

"They tell us in our group that unless we quit smoking we won't please God." Each man nodded. After the recitation of convictions, and prisons, and now this personal failing—this addiction—common among them, the shame in the room was suffocating. "We done enough wrong already, for one lifetime. None of us got any interest in carrying it into the next life."

Each man stared at me unblinking. Each had his hands folded in his lap, but none were at ease—each slowly gripped and ground his fingers together. The stakes were high. Hope for spiritual approval hung for each by a gossamer thread attached to the man sitting on the green, Naugahyde couch encased in plastic.

"Carl's been listening to what you've got to say. Says you're worth asking." Billy looked left and right. They were in agreement. "Can you tell us how to quit smoking?"

As if on cue, all five leaned forward and rested their tattooed forearms on their knees, yellow fingers interlaced into fists. Ten eyes bored into me, five brows furrowed, intent. Something, anything.

I said, "Well, smoking is a hard problem. I appreciate you asking for my counsel. Carl, thank you for your endorsement."

Carl nodded. Once. He never moved his eyes from me. No one else diverted their stare either. I figured it was the look learned in a hard environment where a blink was dangerous.

"You should know first that as sons of God, you are accepted by God. Everything He considered wrong with you and your lives, He crucified and buried with Jesus Christ when you became His followers. There isn't anything you can do, including quitting smoking, that will make Him accept you more than He already does, and there's nothing you can do, including not being able to quit smoking, that will cause God to accept you less than He does right this moment. Whatever else you might be, you are totally accepted by your heavenly Father, God."

They continued staring, but each blinked. I had their attention. And the advantage.

"This said, you've asked specifically about how to quit smoking. I assume you've tried everything and failed."

Ever so slightly, each man's shoulders slumped under the weight of his best effort that wasn't good enough.

"A few jobs before the job I've got now, I cleared land for a living and to put myself through school. Each day I went to work with a chainsaw, an axe, and a log chain. When I cut down a tree, I wrapped my chain around its trunk and dragged it behind my truck to the ravine. There, I rolled it over the edge into the ditch.

"When winter came, I noticed that the trees still standing were naked, their leaves littered the ground, but the trees in the ravine, the ones I'd cut down, still had their leaves. Over the course of a few days, I wondered about this—wondered why this was, wondered what caused a tree to drop its leaves, and why.

"So, I examined the standing trees, bent one limb down and then another, examining each branch. I discovered that everywhere there used to be a leaf, there was a tiny bud—shaped like a miniature football, pointed on the end. It was the start of a new leaf—the tree anticipating spring and new life.

"And it occurred to me: The standing trees are alive. The trees in the ditch are dead. I killed them. They still have leaves because I cut them off from their life. The standing trees shed their leaves in advance of new life, when the weather warms, and winter is over. Each bud shoved the dead leaf off its place on the branch.

"My conclusion was this: Dead leaves don't fall off trees. They are pushed off by the life inside the tree.

"So, my counsel to you is this: Stop worrying about trying to quit smoking so you can please God. It's a misguided motive and it will only make the shame of your addiction worse. You're already accepted by God, so quit worrying about a nonissue.

"Smoking is like a dead leaf hanging on your lives. As new men, sons in the family of God, who have the Holy Spirit of God living in you, when the time is right, the life within you—God's life living inside you—will blossom and empower you to shove the dead leaf of smoking off your life.

"As to motive: Quit trying to do this in your own strength. Quit listening to the bad counsel in your group. Let the life in you do this in you and through you. Trust me. Like the trees in the woods, you'll know when the time is right to drop this dead leaf."

They stared at me. Bored holes into me, not for something more, but confirming the budding hope they felt. I didn't dare avert my eyes from their gaze. The pause seemed an eternity to me, but these were men accustomed to solitary, acquainted with failure, mistakes, rash decisions, dashed hopes, and silent cells echoing every breath and each tick of an interminable clock.

Once they had vetted their thoughts, they looked at one another. Nodded ever-so-slightly.

Billy looked at Carl, and as he nodded, said, "Carl."

Carl stood and moved his chair to make a way to the door for me. The others stood and formed a line for me to follow. Our meeting was over.

I stood, awkwardly aware of not knowing what to do with my hands, or unused pleasantries, or the societal customs from my world so foreign in this one. Each man shook my hand, held it a moment longer than normal, searched my eyes for the measure of me, and once satisfied, said, "Thank you," and let go of my hand.

I walked to the front door. Looked back at the cluster of ex-cons watching, each transformed by the mercy of God, each filled with the life of Christ. I nodded—just once—and as though a dawn arose, they smiled, wry and crooked grins, hopeful based upon the life within.

The lights of Los Angeles twinkled in the far distance. The narrow ribbon of black road waited for the Oldsmobile. I slipped in beside Carl. He watched as I fastened my seatbelt. When it clicked, he looked at me for a long, unnerving moment. Nodded once.

Questions for Consideration

1. How do you think it's possible for men like Carl, Billy, Tom, Johnny, and Mike to be Christians after all they've done?

2. How is it possible for a person to have an ongoing sin—like smoking, or another addiction, or porn—and still be a Christian?

3. What do you think about the remedy Preston offered to Carl and his buddies to stop smoking? What more should he have offered them in the way of proactive counsel?

CHAPTER 23

CAPITAL

You can't spend what you don't have. If you try, it will cost you, compromise you, or deplete you.

This is true for money, time, and your soul. Of these three, money is the most objective, time the most universal, and your soul the most valuable.

So, you budget your money. This means you take inventory of all your needs (food, fun, charitable giving, clothes, car, etc.), quantify the cost of each, and assign that amount of money to each category. If there is not enough money to fully fund each category, you either get another or better job, or you cut your budget until your costs and your money balance. If you have money left over, you invest it for later.

Here's a scenario: If you budget $100 for food and spend $120 at the grocery, you have to borrow from another account to pay the food bill. Let's say you take the $20 overage out of your fun budget. While you cover the overrun in food, you must decline to go out for pizza on Saturday because you don't have the money in your fun budget.

Of course, you're unhappy about not going out on Saturday. So, because you don't have the money in your fun budget, you decide you'll put Saturday night on your credit card. You have a great time.

The credit card bill comes due and because you used it to buy a dinner you didn't have money for—and do not have money for—you can't pay the bill in full and elect to pay the minimum amount due. You repeat the same strategy next week.

Your plan works for a while. It's easy money and you promise to pay the credit card off this summer. Each month, the minimum amount due on the credit card increases for two reasons: 1) You've paid more bills/expenses with your credit card, and 2) the credit card company is adding 20% interest to your balance due.

While a simplistic explanation—it's actually worse than I convey—here's how this works: You owe $100 on your credit card. The credit card company charges you 20% interest for the privilege of delaying to pay off your credit card bill. Let's do the math: 20% of $100 is $20. So, you now owe $120, not $100. Next month, the company charges you 20% on $120. Now you owe them $144, then $173, and then $208—and this is if you leave your bill at $100 and don't spend another dollar of credit. Pretty quickly, your credit card cost is unsustainable.

To recover financially, you must take drastic action, e.g. restructuring debt, finding a second or third job, dropping out of school, selling your car, a family austerity plan. You need big money right away. Drastic problems require drastic actions.

It's a sorry way to live.

Working your way out of financial debt, especially credit card debt, is onerous. The sacrifice is yeoman and the internal shame substantial—all because you tried to spend what you didn't have.

The protection against this nightmare is simple: make a budget, tweak the numbers until you get them right, and then do NOT overspend your budget. As your income increases, i.e. you have more money, you can adjust your budget, but aggressively save money as part of your regular budget. Do this now with your money, and keep doing this, and one of these days (barring something outlandish happening) you will retire without financial worries.

Now that you comprehend financial budgeting, time management works the same way. The only difference between time and money is that everyone has different quantities of money but the same volume of time.

The wise person sits down and assesses what he wants to do—what he wants to accomplish—with his time.

Believe it or not, life only gets more demanding as it unfolds. College is the least demanding period, but in some ways, the easier one to evaluate. Mismanage your time playing video games or scrolling through your device and something will not get done. You'll cram for a test, produce a marginal paper, skim a text, settle for a lower grade and congratulate yourself that you got by. Or when you get older, you'll miss reading, connecting, bonding; you'll marginalize your health, compromise time with your kids, and justify your resulting hostility as justifiable given all that's on you.

Life looks something like this: Your boss requires nine hours. Your commute eats up two more. Exercise is another hour. Eating consumes three or four more hours and sleeping demands eight.

In this scenario, 23-24 hours of your day are gone. You've not gone to the grocery, the dry cleaner, nor have you stopped to get the oil changed in the truck. That must happen on Saturday. Get older. Get married. Add kids, and a dog, and a yard to be tended, and you and your spouse are hunting for ten, tired minutes somewhere to have quick sex.

So, here's the question: Is the time management portrayed the way you wish to manage your time? If so, fine. If not, now you know why thinking this through is important.

Here's the deal: If you are not honest in evaluating the question, thus managing your time with both eyes wide open about life, then you destine yourself to borrow time to pay for time you spent elsewhere.

In the financial world, this looks like debt. In time management, this looks like sleeping six hours, not eight, exercising three days, not six, ignoring the dog, carrying-in your meals, putting your kids in front of a device, and resenting how fast life goes by.

The fallout of poor time management is just as disastrous as credit card debt. Neither are sustainable. A budget is the key.

By now, you've got the picture so I don't have to belabor the point. Still, you need to know that your soul—your mind, your emotions, your character, your choices, your personality—is organized just like a monetary budget and a time management strategy.

Inside your soul there are accounts for love, acceptance, security, self-esteem, personal worth, significance, outlook, connection, and so forth. Just like your monetary budget, you have to fund each account, maintain a healthy balance, and realize that if you deplete an account, you borrow from another account.

For example: You have a boyfriend, let's say. He's a good guy. You have fun together going to the football game, meeting to study, eating together on Friday evenings, and so forth. Let's also say the university paired you with the roommate from hell. She's sarcastic, demanding, a slob, inconsiderate, smells bad, snores, is rude, and does disgusting things in your room.

What are you going to do?

To begin with, you are going to complain about your roommate to your boyfriend. When a new episode transpires, you call your boyfriend and vent. Then, afterward, you debrief with him. Until the poison of your roommate is purged, you call upon your boyfriend to help you bear the burden.

In actuality, what's happening is that your roommate is drawing upon the patience account inside your soul. In turn, you are drawing upon the goodwill account inside your boyfriend's soul. Continue these withdrawals of soul capital for a few weeks and those accounts will be depleted.

By the end of the semester, your patience account with your roommate is bankrupt. And, unless you and your boyfriend have been diligent to invest in his goodwill account, he will be distancing from you and you will be off balance.

Whether it's money, time, or your soul, each account must be managed wisely.

In finance, you respect your budget and invest in savings.

In time, you manage screens, sleep, solitude, and establish productive goals with due-by dates.

Within your soul, you guard the wellsprings of life by what you listen to, what you read, who you spend time with, and reliance upon God to secure your well-being.

A wise man wrote, "Watch over your heart with all diligence. For from it flow the springs of life."[101]

Questions for Consideration

1. This chapter proposes that you budget your money, your time, and your soul. How do you feel about the concept?

2. What prevents you, or impedes you, in each area illustrated?

3. What things reinvest capital into your personal soul most effectively and efficiently?

---

101 Cf. Proverbs 4:23. NASB.

Chapter 24

COMPOSURE

Unless you drive an ambulance or fight fires, there are not many true emergencies in life. Neither is much of life black or white.

Consequently, be suspicious of people who paint the world categorically with only two colors. The better part of wisdom is the composure to let a situation develop.

If a relational bridge needs to be burned, it will be obvious, and for the record, a difference of opinion does not rise to the level of bridge burning. Affiliation with an opposing political party is not just cause for burning a bridge. Even a divorce is not reason to burn a bridge.

Let the situation develop. People are fluid. Relationships ebb and flow. There are always extenuating circumstances you are not privy to knowing.

Seek to understand before you seek to be understood.

God gave you two ears and one mouth. His design intent is clear: Listen twice as much as you talk. Rarely does anything in a relationship rise to the level of an emergency and not much about people is categorical.

My mentor, Mr. Drucker, taught me a rule about confrontation that has served my composure well: If I have something positive to say, I put it in writing. If I have something negative to say, I *never* put it in writing. I always say it personally—face-to-face, in person, not on a video chat.[102]

It takes a lot of composure to abide by this rule, but it keeps you honest and creates the desired outcome. In the end, you want a person to parse every word of praise you give, but you only want them to get the gist of your critique. This leaves both of you in the best possible position to bridge your communication and maintain your composure.

People are multifaceted and life occurs in living color. Composure allows you to engage, appreciate, invest, enjoy, develop, and live fully human.

A good model is Jesus Christ. He insisted on living life to its fullest. He always had the grit of humanity under His fingernails and consistently engaged life by going into the places where life was being ground out.

---

102 Much of my professional life has been spent on the road. I've worked all over the United States, Europe, etc. As is true in all work environments, the inevitable conflicts arose. If I have a conflict with a colleague, I deal with it in person, but that's not a reasonable option if my colleague is in Budapest. If at all possible, face-to-face is best, followed by video, followed by phone, followed by a very short email or letter. Then, the next time we are together in-person, I bring the conflict up to be certain it was resolved by the earlier effort that was not in-person. The principle is this: When something is in writing, the recipient parses every word repeatedly. I want someone to parse every word of affirmation I give. I want someone to get the spirit of a confrontation.

In the end, the categorical thinkers crucified Christ. But even in death, Christ didn't lose composure. He said to the repentant criminal crucified beside Him, "Today you shall be with me in Paradise." And to those bartering for His only possession, His one garment of clothing, He prayed, "Father, forgive them; for they do not know what they are doing."[103]

Questions for Consideration

1. Think of an example or two of how you let the situation develop—or failed to do so. How did these work out and what's your takeaway from this principle of life?

2. What do you think about the principle Mr. Drucker taught of writing praise and speaking confrontation? How does this principle guide you about interacting on Facebook, Twitter, Instagram, email, or any other written or distant medium?

3. If people are multifaceted, and not much in life is black or white, how do you know when to confront? Do you ever strive to be tolerant in all things?

---

103 Cf. Luke 23:43 and 23:34 respectively. NASB.

CHAPTER 25

GOING THROUGH HELL

They say when you are going through hell to keep going. I would add: and walk like you own the place.

You could mistake me as being flippant about hardship, the devil, and spiritual concerns. Please don't. I respect hardship, challenges, and all things associated with hell both literal and figurative.

But respect is neither acquiescence nor fear.

This chapter is about grit and determination. It's about spit in the eye of your adversary. It's about being stood up against the gates of hell and not backing down.[104]

---

104 Cash, Johnny. "I Won't Back Down." *American III: Solitary Man*. Written by Tom Petty, 1989. <https://www.youtube.com/watch?v=N8i5NLyXZdc>. Accessed, 25 April 2020.

Angela Duckworth,[105] a psychologist and researcher, says grit is passion and perseverance for long term, meaningful goals. Grit is about direction, determination, commitment, and not quitting. Grit has nothing to do with talent and everything to do with attitude.

Winston Churchill said in a speech, "Never give in, never give in, never, never, never, never—in nothing, great or small, large or petty—never give in except to convictions of honor and good sense."[106]

People like Ms. Duckworth have spent their lives studying grit. Prime Minister Churchill had to summon courage (grit) when all seemed lost for his country.

What produces grit in one person and not another remains mysterious, but I offer one observation for your consideration: Your next step, or upcoming meeting, or concern—the next thing that has your attention—whether going to university, or revising your family's schedule, or embarking on a major project might not be the most courageous thing you do in life, but it is the next courageous step in your path. Whatever is before you, there is likely a sense that its demands will require grit and a determined resolve.

Failing to engage—do the next, right thing—failing to turn your face to the storm, failing to get back up, and to never quit is about fearing for yourself and

---

105 Duckworth, Angela. *Grit: The Power of Passion and Perseverance*. Scribner. New York, NY. May 2016. *AngelaDuckworth.com*. <https://angeladuckworth.com/grit-book/>. Accessed, 25 April 2020. Also, *TED.com*. May 2013. <https://www.ted.com/talks/angela_lee_duckworth_grit_the_power_of_passion_and_perseverance>. Accessed, 25 April 2020.

106 Churchill, Winston. "Never Give In, Never, Never, Never, 1941." *National Churchill Museum.org*. 2020. <https://www.nationalchurchillmuseum.org/never-give-in-never-never-never.html>. Accessed, 25 April 2020.

what might become of you. You could be embarrassed. You could be outed. You could be a laughing stock. You could be hurt. You could be dismissed, disrespected, disliked, or dissed for the duration.

High stakes indeed!

Here's my observation about what cuts through the noise and keeps you walking even though hell is trying its best to bring you down: Your life is not your own to treasure.

There are shining examples everywhere of people possessed with grit who achieved remarkable outcomes, but none is clearer than the military or first responder. When asked why they behaved heroically, most say something like, "I'm not a hero. I was just doing my job. However, I work in the company of heroes."

What these people are telling us is that they are called to a task. They have dedicated their life to preserving life for others under the harshest and hardest of circumstances. We speak of them as laying down their lives so others can live. So, when all hell breaks loose, they march into it like they own the place.

I can make the same argument about relationships. Take marriage, for example: There are lines in the traditional ceremony that each party pledges to honor until nothing short of death separates them. If you think about it, marriage is pledging to live a life of sacrifice, not reward.

Life takes grit. As you add others to your life, life becomes grittier. Being a good friend takes more grit than living alone. Married life takes yet more grit. Parental life takes more grit even yet.

Apprehending a determined life is about taking the next challenging step. Then, the next, and the next. Grit achieves incremental goals on the way to gaining an ultimate goal. Big, audacious goals are comprised of gritty next steps.

Stepping into a new place takes grit. College is incredibly exciting. It's also terrifying. For most, going away to college is the same as being shoved out of the nest. You either fly or you crash and burn.

I would lie if I told you college wasn't a grand adventure. It's a fantastic time! Maybe the best years of your life. But I would also lie if I told you life gets easier from this point forward. It doesn't. It gets harder in many ways.

Making your own money. Starting a new job. Getting married. Raising a child. Buying a house. Being promoted. All amazing adventures in life's journey. All demand perseverance, persistence, and determination.

Grit.

I'm not saying life is a living hell, but I know of no one in whose life some rain did not fall, some storms did not rage, and some challenges did not arise that caused them to fear greatly.

Determining to take the next step in life based upon your circumstances means you will fail to step. Grit is not defined circumstantially. Grit is defined by determining to step.

Running away, turning back, blaming, denying, rationalizing, projecting, seeking revenge, growing bitter, anesthetizing your brain with alcohol or drugs, sidestepping into sex, or lies, or the easy path…. These are all poisons to your soul. Tolerate them and they are poisons to your life.

You have one life to live. You're into it knee deep when you are in your early twenties. By the time your mid-twenties arrive, you're swimming with the sharks. Swim scared or swim with determination. One way or the other, you're going swimming.

Whether literal or figurative, hell is measured in degrees. The same is true of grit.

Hell can happen. We call it, all hell breaking loose. Failure. Death. Divorce. Betrayal. The house floods. The insurance company won't pay. Duplicity. Deceit. You have little-to-no control over when or how hell breaks loose, but you have absolute control over how you respond. This is true throughout life.

There's a Christian perspective on grit that I find helpful: As a follower of Jesus Christ, I have given all that I am to Him in exchange for all that He is through me and in me. A line from Saint Paul's writings is my motto: "To me to live is Christ, and to die is gain."[107]

If my life is not my own, i.e. my life belongs to God, then regardless of hell, high water, or sunshine, I possess the courage to live with focused abandon.

I've lived long enough to realize that going through hell is not for the faint of heart.

But!

I believe I have what it takes. I have the Spirit of God Himself living in me. His life is mine. He has promised to do good by me. I trust Him. Step after step, He is faithful and I am determined. This is the dance He and I do and this is how I define grit.

---

107 Philippians 1:21. NASB.

So, when I'm focused and am playing my "A game," I say to myself: "Preston, let life rock and roll, buddy. Lift up your head, stick out your chest. Fix your eyes on Jesus. Hell could not hold Him and it can't hold you."

Questions for Consideration

1. Do you believe all people either possess grit or can obtain grit? Do some people not have grit? Do some people not need grit?

2. Are you born with grit or is it developed? Can you get more grit, and if so, from where, by what means?

3. Can you manage your life in such fashion so as to not need grit—or to need less than if you do not manage your life? What are the implications for your next steps in life?

CHAPTER 26

CROUCHING DRAGON

"I believe that there is one story in the world, and only one, that has frightened and inspired us, so that we live in a Pearl White[108] serial of continuing thought and wonder. Humans are caught—in their lives, in their thoughts, in their hungers and ambitions, in their avarice and cruelty, and in their kindness and generosity too—in a net of good and evil. I think this is the only story we have and that it occurs on all levels of feeling and intelligence. There is no other story." –John Steinbeck[109]

The quote is from *East of Eden*. Steinbeck considered the book his *magnum opus*, his most important work as a writer. The one story he references and explores is the story of Cain and Abel.

---

108 Pearl White was an actress who starred in film serials.

109 Steinbeck, John. *East of Eden*. Penguin Books. New York, NY. 1952. P. 411.

Three times Steinbeck recreates the biblical story of the two brothers and the struggle between good and evil. Each iteration concludes in keeping with the original, "Then Cain went out from the presence of the Lord, and settled in the land of Nod, east of Eden."[110]

The crux of the biblical story is Genesis 4:7. Cain is angry with God. His brother, Abel, stands between him and the object of his anger.

God speaks to Cain, "If you do well, will not your countenance be lifted up? And if you do not do well, sin is crouching at the door; and its desire is for you, but you must master it."[111]

The message is graphic: Cain, you have a choice. Choose poorly, and sin will consume you.

Even though the fall of mankind and banishment from the Garden of Eden have already occurred, verse 4:7 is the first mention of sin in the Bible. It is written as a noun, not a verb. Sin is "a person, place, or thing" in its first mention, not the verbal action of a shortfall.

The King James translation of the Bible captures the gender given to sin in the original language of the Bible: "If thou doest well, shalt thou not be accepted? And if thou doest not well, sin lieth at the door. And unto thee shall be his desire, and thou shalt rule over him."[112]

---

110 Genesis 4:16. NASB.

111 Genesis 4:7. NASB.

112 Genesis 4:7. *Holy Bible. Authorized King James Version* (KJV).

Grammatically, both "it" or "him" are accurate translations. Either renders a sobering reality: Sin is personified. Sin possesses capacity. He has essence and being. Sin is viable. He calculates, strategizes, positions, waits, and crouches—"lieth" like a stalking cat—hunting an opportunity, pursuing prey. Sin is the personification of evil, and evil intent; of evil demonstrating malice of forethought; of a living evil portrayed later in the Bible as a "great, red dragon."[113] And he must be mastered.

Paraphrasing: Cain, don't lose focus at this critical juncture. You have a choice. If you choose good, your outlook will improve. If you fail to choose good, there is a crouching dragon called sin lying in wait at the door of your soul. His intent and purpose are to possess you. It's a crucial moment. Cain, you must master sin.

Choose well, and do good. Choose poorly, and be consumed by evil. "Humans are caught—in their lives, in their thoughts, in their hungers and ambitions, in their avarice and cruelty, and in their kindness and generosity too—in a net of good and evil," quoting Steinbeck again.

"You must master it (sin)" the New American Standard translation reads. "You must rule over it" the English Standard Version reads. "Thou shalt rule over him" King James translated.

"You must," "you must." It's imperative to Cain's well-being that he choose good. Evil lies crouching, waiting at the door to his soul.

---

113 Revelation 12:3. NASB.

"Thou shalt." It is clear what Cain *must* do, but what he *will* do is not yet known.

For all the force of the imperative translation, "you must," and the possibility of the future translation, "thou shalt," it remains to be seen what Cain will choose to do.

Speculation. Doubt. Uncertainty. Anticipation.

Cain may choose to rule over sin. Or, Cain may choose not to rule over sin.

The story of humankind is short—only sixteen verses. Genesis 4:8, "And it came about when they were in the field, that Cain rose up against Abel his brother and killed him."[114] Eight verses later, Cain leaves the presence of the Lord and settles in Nod, east of Eden.

"Thou shalt." "You must." In the original Hebrew text, this phrase is a single word, *timshel*: Thou may (or thou mayest not)—rule over him.

"We have only one story. All novels, all poetry, are built on the never-ending contest in ourselves of good and evil. And it occurs to me that evil must constantly respawn, while good, while virtue, is immortal. Vice has always a new fresh young face, while virtue is venerable as nothing else in the world is," Steinbeck writes later.[115]

---

114 Genesis 4:8. NASB.

115 Steinbeck, John. Ibid. P. 413.

Like Cain, you and I have a choice. We possess the ability to determine our countenance, to change our countenance, by the choice we make.

We may or we may not.

Over several thousand years, the Bible records the flow of human history in poetry, novel, history, and biography. The clash between good and evil is the recurring theme. If it were any less human, we might lay the text aside given dark passages similar to Genesis 4:1-16. But we keep reading for the same reason we continue reading any other piece of riveting literature: We want to know how the story works out.

The crouching dragon of sin is featured once again in the Book of Romans, written by the Apostle Paul hundreds of years after Genesis was penned. He laments, "But sin, taking opportunity through the commandment, produced in me coveting of every kind; for apart from the Law sin is dead."[116]

Over the course of this dark chapter, Paul describes the tortured, internal ebb and flow of one of the greatest battles between good and evil ever written. It is so dark, so demoralizing, and so defeating that many theologians attribute Romans chapter 7, not to Paul the Apostle, but to Paul before he became a follower of Jesus Christ, the man known as Saul the Pharisee. These theologians are moralizing.

Paul's battle is no different than Cain's, no different than yours, and no different than mine. The question is not whether Saul or Paul wrote Romans

---

116 Romans 7:8. NASB.

7. The question is what did the man see during his struggle? What's the outcome? Is there help for you and me in our contention with good and evil?

The recounting of Paul's experience spans four chapters of Romans, chapters 5-8. What Paul conveys in his writing that we don't see in Cain's experience is the internal dynamic of the conflict—what's transpiring within Paul while he decides whether he will rule over sin or not, and if he makes the attempt, what resources does he have to win the day. The outcome of failure is stark and the good-evil tension palpable across four chapters.

There is no other story for us, only the one. What Paul does that Genesis does not, and that Steinbeck only hints of, is to take us deeper into the story of humanity and introduce us to two kinds of men, each compromised by the battle between good and evil, just as all men are, but each man possessing a different approach to the battle and his story.

Come the day of conflict, the first man's approach and resource is himself. Alone, the captain of his fate, he may or may not summon the internal strength to overcome the crouching dragon. The record of this man's endeavor litters the epochs of human civilization.

The second man, the spiritual man as Paul identifies him—when the day of battle comes, is equally compromised and the stakes are just as great. His question is common to all warriors preparing to engage the cunning enemy of sin: When the smoke clears, whose will I be? Will I be on the side of good with my heart resolute or will my countenance be downcast and I succumbed to evil, mauled by the crouching dragon, captured, incarcerated in his maw?

Reflecting on his experience in the day of conflict, Paul identifies himself as a spiritual man and notes he has two advantages over the independent man. First, Paul recognizes he is not alone. He declares that he is indwelt by the Spirit of God to whom he has declared allegiance and upon whom he is depending. Second, because he has been made a new person through faith in Jesus Christ, he identifies a new heart for the battle, and a deep desire to rule over sin and master him.

Then, stepping onto the field and engaging his foe, Paul describes and conveys a brutal battle between good and evil. He is caught between the force of light and the dark force of sin. Chapter 7 is torturous, disconsolate, and demoralizing literature.

But Paul's conflict with the crouching dragon that lies in wait has a different ending than Cain's conflict with sin. Whereas Cain chose evil, Paul chose good.

Both men faced the same battle: good versus evil. Both were stalked by the same foe: the crouching dragon of sin. Both faced the same choice: Will I rule or be ruled?

In both stories, like your own, the crux is conveyed in one word: *timshel*.

You may.

A Book Recommendation: *No Mercy*

No Mercy[117] is a sweeping adventure of life, love, trust, and desire—an odyssey asserting that life is more than meets the eye. It is the story of good and evil, of spirit versus flesh, and the battle engaged by Hank Henderson to survive and emerge victorious.

No Mercy is a novel that I wrote to portray—and reveal— the major players in the spiritual battle between the forces of darkness and God, the High King of Glory.

Sin is portrayed in the character, Jester. Magician is the Holy Spirit, Vassar is Jesus, and the King is God. Hank is you. You can purchase *No Mercy* wherever fine books are sold—including Amazon.

Questions to Consider

1. Apocryphal or real? The stuff of a work from fiction or an accurate portrayal of life? Is the crouching dragon mythological, metaphorical, or real?

2. What emotion rises up within your soul when you consider the crouching dragon?

3. What do you make of the choice? Timshel. You may (or you may not).

---

117 Gillham, Preston. *No Mercy.* Bonefish Publication. Fort Worth, TX. 2010. *Amazon.com.* <https:// www.amazon.com/No-Mercy-Preston-Gillham/dp/0984510303>. Accessed, 25 April 2020.

CHAPTER 27

FORGIVING

"Let us forget and forgive injuries," Cervantes wrote in *Don Quixote*.[118]

"But if you do not forgive others," Jesus said during His most famous sermon, "then your Father [God] will not forgive your transgressions."[119]

"The first to apologize is the bravest. The first to forgive is the strongest. The first to forget is the happiest." Author unknown, but one tying happiness directly to your successful forgetfulness of a wrong done to you.

Once you have forgotten, you will know you have forgiven. Until then, keep trying to forget. Which is problematic if you yourself are in need of forgiveness from God—and who among us has not offended God? It's no wonder we are not happy.

---

118 Cervantes, Miguel de. *Don Quixote*. Translated by Tobias Smollett. Dover Publications. New York, NY. 2018.

119 Matthew 6:15. NASB.

My parents never forgot December 7, 1941, just as President Franklin Roosevelt predicted when he pronounced it, "a date which will live in infamy."[120] The Japanese bombing of Pearl Harbor plunged the United States formally into World War II. Dad was at Okinawa. Uncle Bill was a tail gunner in a B-17. He was shot down and walked back to England three times. They never forgot.

My friends born after 1990 will never forget September 11, 2001—the terrorist attacks on the United States of America. Twenty years of war—and counting—ensued. On the anniversary of the attacks, our ongoing national resolve appears on banners, in print, voiced, and via media, "Never forget!"

I will never forget the day my wife left, the day her divorce papers arrived in the mail, or the day I removed my wedding ring. "The holiest of all holidays are those / Kept by ourselves in silence and apart; / The secret anniversaries of the heart, / When the full river of feeling overflows."[121] There's no forgetting in these lines by Longfellow.

By now, you have accumulated offenses that are forever etched into the walls of your soul. You can no more forget your betrayal, your sexual assault, your dad's drunken rampages, your mom's slap across your face, or your brother's suicide than you can forget your name.

---

120 Library of Congress. "Speech by Franklin D. Roosevelt, New York (Transcript)." *LoC.gov*. December 8, 1941.

121 Longfellow, Henry Wadsworth. "Holidays." *Poets.org*. <https://poets.org/poem/holidays>. Accessed, 1 May 2020.

Should my chapter end now? Is forgiveness a fantasy because forgetting isn't possible? Is happiness forever elusive? Is freedom from your wrong as likely as elephants flying?

No. I would not have begun this chapter if I did not believe there is an alternative angle to consider about forgiveness and forgiving.

Trying mightily to forget will only sear into your memory the wrong. I disagree with Cervantes—and all the others who repeat the pithy admonition to "forgive and forget" as if it is realistic, desirable, wise, and practical. I believe you can forgive—genuinely, sincerely forgive—and still remember. In fact, a truly great offense should be remembered.

This means that I believe happiness is possible. In truth, happiness is a choice, not a by-product.

To make sense of Jesus' teaching about a conditional forgiveness—the if-then of "if you forgive, then you will be forgiven"—you must understand the larger point of His sermon, commonly called, the Sermon on the Mount.[122] In the same sermon, He said that if a man has ever lusted sexually in his thoughts, then he has committed adultery,[123] and if he has ever been angry, he has committed murder.[124] Speaking about social conduct, He said that you must be perfect in the same way and degree that God is perfect.[125]

---

122 Cf.: Matthew 5-7. NASB.

123 Matthew 5:27-28. NASB.

124 Matthew 5:21-24. NASB.

125 Matthew 5:48. NASB.

By the time Jesus concluded His sermon, every person in attendance would have been overwhelmed by the impossibility of ever pleasing God. Whatever rationale Jesus' listeners were using to justify their lives, Jesus buried their hopes with His teaching.

His point and purpose were to utterly defeat everyone's notion of being approved and accepted by God based upon their performance. Simply, He wanted His listeners to be so defeated and demoralized that they would have no rebuttal, no self-defense. Their only recourse would be, "Jesus, is there any way to get to God?" To which He would reply, "Yes, I'm the way to God. I've come to make it possible to be accepted by God, but acceptance with God will not be by your performance. It is through Me and Me alone."[126]

So you see, Jesus' conditional forgiveness is an impossibility, nestled among many other impossibilities, to intentionally jerk His listeners away from their preconceptions and misconceptions and examine Him as "the way, the truth, and the life."[127] To build a belief about how forgiveness works based upon this teaching is misguided and a recipe for utter failure, demoralization, bondage, and frustration as you attempt to forgive those who wound you.

There are many offenses in the world, many wrongs, and no human being without scars. God indicates in the Bible that all of this sinfulness is an offense to Him, a personal wrong, a wound that He must manage.[128]

---

126 Cf.: John 14:6. NASB.

127 Ibid.

128 Cf.: Isaiah 53. NASB.

So, how does God forgive? What's His formula—and possibly your template?

God says in the Bible, "I, even I, am the one who wipes out your transgressions for My own sake."[129] St. Paul says something similar, appearing to emulate God's formula for forgiveness. He writes, "I determined this for my own sake, that I would not come to you in sorrow again."[130]

Both God and Paul decided to forgive because it was in their best interest to do so.

In other words, forgiveness is something you do for yourself, not for the person who offended you.

Forgiveness is not about forgetting, granting absolution, or considering the offense to be like water gone under the bridge. In forgiving, you grant yourself freedom—which means you're now free to focus on other things. Not today, or the next day, or probably the next, but in time, as you think about other things, the offense will not own your soul's attention. Something else will have become as positively powerful to you as the offense was negatively hurtful.

You can engage the powerful work of forgiveness all by yourself. In fact, you can forgive whether the person who offended you ever apologizes or not.

You can forgive someone—or a group of folks—who offend you, and who you may not have ever met. You can forgive a movement. You can forgive a period in history and all associated with it. You can forgive a government.

---

129 Isaiah 43:25. NASB.

130 2 Corinthians 2:1. NASB.

You can even forgive a dead person.

Forgiveness is a choice you make for yourself.

The choice of forgiveness uproots the offense that can give rise to bitterness, resentment, and hatred if left untended. Grasping forgiveness establishes a protective boundary around your soul and eliminates the foothold of harm done against you.

Choosing forgiveness is a determination to live differently, to live beyond, to not languish underneath a wrong perpetrated against you.

Choosing to forgive—for your own sake—is a decision to model your response to ungraciousness foisted against you after the model demonstrated by God.

Alternatively, if you harbor an offense against you, whether for revenge, hatred, or as your just due, you join your offender in bringing destruction into your world. Choosing not to forgive is self-destructive. "Not forgiving is like drinking rat poison and then waiting for the rat to die," says Anne Lamott.[131]

Forgiveness is a gift God gave to Himself for His own good. He models it for us through Scripture and grants the power of forgiveness to us. It is an act of self-care, freeing us from the ongoing tyranny of the offense thrust upon us.

Choosing to forgive moves you forward. Beyond the offense. Past your offender. It sets you free.

---

131 Lamott, Anne. *Traveling Mercies.* Audio book narrated by, Rebecca Lowman. Penguin. New York, NY. 2000.

Notice, I have not written to you about apologies, confrontation, or reconciliation. These are associated with forgiveness, but forgiveness is not dependent upon them. So, I'll leave these for another day.

Personally, here's how I implement forgiveness:

1) I assess my wound. A scratch is different than a gaping hole. With assessment, I'm seeking to honor my wound accordingly. It's unwise to suffer a wound and dismiss it as nothing. It's petty to scream over a scratch. Proper assessment indicates the degree of labor necessary to forgive effectively. Forgiving a friend who unintentionally hurts your feelings requires a different degree of forgiveness than the hardship of forgiving your dead uncle who sexually assaulted you or the spouse who persistently berates you.

2) As a Christian, my faith teaches me that God wants me to cast my cares upon Him.[132] In other words, God wants to, a) give me a place to put my concerns, b) be with me as I choose to forgive, and c) help me adopt a healthy focus that is to my benefit. So, the second thing I do after assessment is, I envision the person who hurt me. They could be dead. It doesn't matter. I bring them before my consciousness, and deliberately acknowledge that God is with me and in me, i.e. I'm not alone, I say—and by "say" I mean, I may think my way through, I may verbalize aloud in a private place, I may write in my journal—my grievance and my choice to forgive. "Today, with God as my witness and support, Uncle Joe, I forgive you for the fear you brought into my childhood, the loss of innocence...." "I forgive you for failing as a Board of Directors, for betraying me, misrepresenting me...." "Nancy, I forgive you for

---

132 Cf.: Matthew 11:28-30; 1 Peter 5:6-7. NASB.

the terrible curses you leveled at me in God's name, for telling me I'm stupid and dumb...." Name the person and the offense. Once I've done a detailed and systematic forgiveness, I pray something like this: "Father God, you know the offense and you've heard my decision to forgive. I give my uncle, the Board of Directors, my brother, my mother—whoever and whatever—to you to do with as you see fit. Now, please help me redirect my attention to healing and self-care."

3.) If there are lessons to be learned from the experience, I note those. There's no sense in wasting a sorrow or failing to learn from a mistake.

4.) I next choose—sometime relentlessly choose and choose and choose—to redirect myself and my thoughts. I may go outside and work in the yard, go for a bike ride, sit on the patio, read a book, listen to my special playlist called, "Mine!", or go back to work. Last week, I chopped wood until I could barely heft the axe again. The offense and the offender will cross my mind a hundred times, a thousand times, and each time I reference my forgiveness and turn my determination back to the subject I'm refocusing on. In time, the offense is managed and my soul's equilibrium returned.

The world is a rough and tumble place. It always has been. Being a peacemaker, or turning the other cheek, or going along, or being easy, or deferential—my observation is that you can't escape the fallout of others' poor choices. Sooner or later, you must practice forgiveness or be owned by bitterness.

I suffered a wound last week that was alarming in its intended severity. It scared me, in fact. I've forgiven my attacker, but am not finished navigating the fallout. That's another thing I've learned: I can forgive up front, right away, and let the situation play itself out.

I've learned that the more I have practiced forgiveness, the better I've gotten at effectively and efficiently forgiving. Sometimes, it's more prudent to forgive in bite-sized decisions than the whole enchilada at once.

Last night I sat for a time and thought about this recent offense. That I sat to reflect doesn't mean I lost my forgiveness or need to try again. It means that I'm laboring over a significant hit to make certain I don't miss something important. I concluded that I don't think my attacker is finished with me. So, as part of being wise, I am calculating how to prepare, to love, to be practical, and what prudence requires of me.

Just because I've forgiven doesn't release me from the due diligence of being shrewd as a serpent and innocent as a dove.[133]

Questions for Consideration

1. If you are unable to forget, how do you protect yourself from bitterness?

2. Why is it important to review a wound? How often do you need to review the wound you need to forgive?

3. Is forgiveness permanent or must it be renewed? What's your rationale?

133 Cf.: Matthew 10:16. NASB.

Chapter 28

PEACE

"Peace cannot be kept by force, it can only be achieved by understanding," said Albert Einstein, one of the men who helped invent the atomic bomb.[134]

Outside of my own soul, I disagree with Einstein. Inside my soul, I agree with Einstein.

In my experience, there are two things that bring me peace: life and death—and clearly, this needs some explanation.

As a Christian, I knew theoretically that I had peace. I have Jesus Christ living in my life and the Bible says He is the Prince of Peace.[135] Therefore, I have peace.

---

134 Einstein, Albert. *Goodreads.com*. <https://www.goodreads.com/quotes/4464-peace-cannot-be-kept-by-force-it-can-only-be>. Accessed, 25 April 2020.

135 Isaiah 9:6; John 14:27. NASB.

Except, I didn't. Not experientially. Until recently.

For most of my six-plus decades on this planet I've had a figurative gun to my head. Pushing. Producing. Calculating. Achieving. Winning. Recovering. Every moment of every day. It was as though my head was full of snakes. Ideas squirming. Calculations slithering. Opportunity lying in wait. Striking. I felt cold blooded.

The Christian peace I had was sound theologically, but daily elusive.

I wrote earlier that I didn't really begin to think critically until I was twenty-one or twenty-two years old. I had lived 25% of my allotted eighty-or-so years. Looking backward now, 80% of my days are spent.

Here's some perspective: If you work hard, and live a balanced life, and do the right things, and dream big, and set audacious goals, and manage your money, and have friends, and do a few other things as well, then you will be successful, people will love you, society will recognize you, and you will have peace. They say. Except life doesn't work this way.

Peace doesn't come from what you do, it comes from the way you view what you do.

The Book of Ecclesiastes in the Bible speaks of "vanity," often translated as meaningless. Literally, the writer is proposing this image: Life is like a vapor. Trying to grasp it, as if to manage it or control it, is a vain effort. In his book, *Living Life Backward*, David Gibson[136] likens life to the rising smoke from

---

136 Gibson, David. *Living Life Backward*. Crossway. Wheaton, IL. 2017. Pp. 20-21.

a candle you've just blown out. Reach out and grasp some smoke. Put it in your pocket for later.

While you can see it, you can't get hold of it. Trying is futile.

The point is: Since life is like a wisp of smoke, trying to grab it is not peaceful; it's frustrating, disillusioning, and the more you try, or the closer you get to the smoke disappearing, the more desperate you are inclined to become.

But the remedy is not so easy as not grasping. Life is not a proposition you walk away from.

So, if you can't control life, and you can't walk away from life, what option remains?

Your other option is altering how you look at life. There are two views: a close look and a distant look.

First, the close look, the daily look, the experience of living life day in, day out, right now. The writer of Ecclesiastes explored life from all its angles: achievement, sex, money, fame, pleasure, and leaving a lasting legacy. In the end, he had two observations: First, nothing he achieved or experienced brought him peace, and second, what he did accomplish was left to another to manage or mismanage after he died.

It sounds depressing, doesn't it? In philosophical terms, it's almost fatalistic.

But, it's not.

You can choose to look at life either pessimistically or optimistically. Pessimism realizes life is not fair, and in the end, you will die, another will manage your affairs, and you will be forgotten. Optimism recognizes the same thing about life but with the perspective that in the end God will make everything right.

All that is wrong in the world, more specifically, your world, will be made right one of these days. Judgment is coming and it will be conducted by a loving, fair, and absolutely good God. There's nothing you can do to escape this, so why not embrace reality, bring your best effort each day, and entrust yourself to God by joining His forever family as one of His children?[137]

When I recognized this viewpoint, I stopped grasping at life's smoke. Oh, I worked just as hard as always, celebrated my achievements, put my name on books, loved my wife, walked my dog, fly fished, smoked a cigar now and then, and drank bourbon on the patio.

Life is to be lived, just not grasped at.

By not grasping, I was free to hold onto God. More accurately, rest in the reality that God is holding onto me.[138]

This is the up-close perspective of living life and finding peace.

---

137 For more insight into becoming a member of God's family, see Appendix A in *Swagger*.

138 Cf. Romans 8:38-39; Hebrews 13:5. NASB. Consider the pledge of God in Hebrews 13:5-6 as translated in the *Amplified Bible*: "Let your character [your moral essence, your inner nature] be free from the love of money [shun greed—be financially ethical], being content with what you have; for He has said, 'I WILL NEVER [under any circumstances] DESERT YOU [nor give you up nor leave you without support, nor will I in any degree leave you helpless], NOR WILL I FORSAKE *or* LET YOU DOWN *or* RELAX MY HOLD ON YOU [assuredly not]!' 6 So we take comfort *and* are encouraged *and* confidently say, 'THE LORD IS MY HELPER [in time of need], I WILL NOT BE AFRAID. WHAT WILL MAN DO TO ME?'" *Biblegateway.com*. <https://www.biblegateway.com/passage/?search=hebrews+13%3A5-6&version=AMP>. Accessed, 25 April 2020.

The distant look, which is equally important to maintain, is this: One of these days, you don't know when, you are going to die. It seems a long way off now, but it is inevitable. In fact, death is the one certainty in life.

Humans live as though they can beat death, but in the end, no one does. You can certainly live a healthy lifestyle and enjoy more days on earth, but you can't escape death.

One of the things that brings happiness to life is living in a responsible way. So, plan for the future. If you want to go skiing in the winter, plan to stay in shape. If you have kids, save money for their education. If you want to enjoy time off, plan and save for vacations and retirement. This only makes sense.

By now, you are old enough to have had friends whose lives were before them, yet they died in a car wreck, or drowned at the lake, or succumbed to cancer. Life seems inevitable, but it's not. When you get to be my age, you will have sat through many funerals and carried more than one coffin to the grave.

Plan for life, but do so responsibly. Since the only constant in life is death, why not take the counsel of Stephen Covey, the business guru, and begin with the end in mind?[139] Consider death and look backwards at how you wish to live. The only mooring in life, the only anchor point, is death.

Use this inescapable truth to your advantage and live the life you desire now as a result.

---

139 Covey, Stephen. *The 7 Habits of Highly Effective People.* Simon & Schuster. New York, NY. 1989. Pp. 95ff.

Some have considered this and determined to eat, drink, and be merry because tomorrow they die. That's fatalism.[140] It's been tried and evaluated. Fatalism leads to unhappiness and no peace.

Peace is yours when you live each day as though it is your last. You are diligent and responsible. You embrace each moment of every day. Some of those moments will be pleasant, some will be sorrowful. Trust God as your heavenly Father. Know with confidence that He will judge and make all things right one of these days.

Live in light of your death and realize peace today.

Questions for Consideration

1. Is there a difference between Christian peace and peace in life?

2. Is this chapter merely about outlook—pessimism versus optimism—or is there more to peace than outlook?

3. What's your understanding of planning how you live by contemplating your death?

---

140 "Fatalism." *Wikipedia.org.* <https://en.wikipedia.org/wiki/Fatalism>. Accessed, 25 April 2020. Also, "Fatalism." *Plato.Stanford.edu.* <https://plato.stanford.edu/entries/fatalism/>. Accessed, 25 April 2020.

Chapter 29

TEARS

Big boys don't cry. Women are more emotional than men. Tears are a weakness. I apologize for crying.

You've heard it all, as have I. Routine thoughts about tears are flippant.

Candidly, it's worse than flippant: they aren't true.

Tears deliver important messages. First among them is, pay attention. Something important is happening, something so important it needs to be squeezed out of my soul through my eyes and cared for. Now. Not later. Thoughtfully.

Given this, denying your tears, wiping them away too quickly, dismissing them, belittling them, justifying them—anything other than recognizing and respecting them, then seeking to understand them, is inappropriate at best, irresponsible at worst.

Why am I crying? What are my tears about? Stay with the question until you answer it. Tears are too important to brush them off.

I see your tears. Would you tell me about them?

I see your tears. Something important is occurring. I'm here.

I see your tears. Thank you for trusting me with them.

Any dismissal of tears says something bad about the person dismissing the tears and virtually nothing about the person crying. As you build your life, surround yourself with people honest enough to cry and faithful enough to treasure your tears. Anyone else is beneath you.

The well-dressed man carries two handkerchiefs. One is typically white and carried in the back pocket of his slacks. This handkerchief is for his use. The second is noticeable. It's a statement. It is carried and worn in the outside, breast pocket of his jacket or suit. This handkerchief is for her. A gentleman understands a woman's tears are important. A wise man knows his tears are important as well.

The Christian perspective on tears is meaningful: Chief among those abusive of your tears is God's enemy, the devil. His abuse is predictable. When you are hurt, he always questions God's faithfulness.

There's an image for what he does: kicking you when you're down.

In truth, God cares deeply about tears. There is a passage in the Book of Psalms that describes God catching every tear you cry and storing it in a bottle. Once done, He carefully considers your tears and writes about them in His journal.[141]

Who else is so faithful and careful with the important things that concern you?

Questions for Consideration

1. Tears are awkward. Uncomfortable to be around. How does this chapter help you step toward tears instead of retreating from them?

2. Are there occasions when you should manage your tears—or someone else's tears? What's an example? Also, are all tears liquid, i.e. they fill your eyes and run down your cheeks? Is it possible to cry internally, i.e. shed no visible tears? If so, should you keep this to yourself or share it with someone trusted?

3. How does it make you feel to realize God saves each tear you shed and notes the occasion upon which it occurred?

---

141 Psalm 56:8. NASB.

Chapter 30

SWAGGER

Years ago, one of my buddies hit a rough patch in his life when his son had a terrible accident.

The young man was a military officer. He and his commanding officer were on their way back to their base after a torturous deployment. Both were exhausted. The commanding officer was asleep in the passenger seat. My buddy's son was driving and fighting to stay awake.

He drifted. The wheels dropped off the roadway into loose gravel. The car skidded, hit a culvert, and flipped end-over-end.

Because the passenger seat was reclined, the commanding officer shot out under his seat belt, through the shattered windshield, and was killed on impact. My friend's son was banged up, but survived. He was charged with manslaughter, would likely do hard time, and his military career was over.

In the end, the young man did not serve time in prison. Of course, his life was altered irrevocably, but he landed okay, all things considered. The two sets of parents became close friends and remain so.

But for many months it was dark and foreboding. During the midst of this, I asked my buddy how he was holding up. He smiled one of those half-cocked smiles people in pain display and said, "I've lost my swagger."

A proper swagger conveys confidence in the cadence of how you carry yourself. An exaggerated swagger telegraphs the opposite of its intention: a lack of confidence. You can't fake a swagger. If you are confident, you will carry yourself as such. If not, you won't.

In my friend's case, when he said he'd lost his swagger, it was his way of telling me his confidence was low.

Life is an interesting proposition. For some reading these lines, college will introduce you to your first challenge. For others, you are well acquainted with hardship. While I suppose it's theoretically possible to find someone who arrives at the end of their days having weathered no storms, I've neither met nor heard about such an individual. If they exist, I can't imagine their soul has much temper to it.

Is it possible to be confident no matter what comes? Is it realistic to believe you can find security that is unshakeable, peace that is unsurpassed, and value that will not diminish?

The obvious answer, or perhaps the apparent answer, to these questions is, No. It's not possible or realistic—to establish any of these things. Look around.

All of us either are or will soon join the ranks of the walking wounded. *C'est la vie* (such is life).

Life has an uncanny way of compromising our sense of well-being. It's a constant maintenance task. All of us struggle—and with each effort we splint the compromise to our well-being with devices of our own design.

If you feel like your worth is lacking, you might buy a new dress or another diamond. If you don't feel loved, you might sleep around. If you question your security, you might vow to be a millionaire by age thirty.

Here's the deal: diamonds, and sex, and a robust portfolio will not supply the deficits in your soul. As wonderful as these things are, they don't possess the capacity to do for you what you require. Love is a need. A diamond is not. Sex is incredible, but it lasts for twenty minutes. Security is essential, your portfolio is as fickle as international relations.

In all candor, money, sex, power, and possessions are the best tools life offers. If this is all that's in your toolbox, good luck.

There is an additional option to consider.

The Bible says that God knows what you need before you even ask Him.[142] It says in another passage that He will supply all your needs, not based upon the world's resources, but from His vast storehouse of riches.[143]

---

142 Matthew 6:8. NASB.

143 Philippians 4:19. NASB.

If God says He will supply all your essential needs as a human being, how foolish is it to attempt to secure fulfillment with anything other than Him?

I'm a fan of diamonds, sex, money, recognition, cars, and nice fly rods. But all of these are simply amenities in life. They are not life itself and won't help my swagger.

As long as I maintain my confidence in God through Jesus Christ, no matter the beating this world dishes out, I may limp, but I'll still have my swagger.

Questions for Consideration

1. *Is a swagger visible or invisible?*

2. *How do you discern between true confidence and false confidence?*

3. *Is it possible to be truly confident—in possession of true confidence— and not be a Christian?*

Chapter 31

SEX

Wow! Just wow! When God invented sex, He outdid Himself. Obviously, He had more in mind than populating the planet.

Years ago, one of my buddies told me about the sex talk with his son. "So pal, since you have two sisters, you understand that your mom and I have had sex three times." The boy nodded. My friend continued, "The truth of the matter is, sometimes your mom and I have sex just for the fun of it." Again, the boy nodded, then said, "I was kind of wondering about that, Dad."

You've probably heard it said, anybody can have sex, not everyone can make love. And you know what? That's true. Not everyone can make love. The implication, which is true as well, is that making love takes practice—a lifetime of practice.

As of this writing, I guesstimate Dianne and I have practiced making love while having sex about five thousand times. I can't begin to estimate how many other ways we have made love together. Walks. Kisses. Dinners. Silence together in the same room. Sharing enchiladas. Laughing. Crying. Touching elbows on the console.

Sex is wonderful. But make sure you understand: Intercourse is rudimentary sex. Making love is complex sex that accesses your sexuality. Done together properly, sex is like relational rocket fuel. Engaged in casually, it's like a cancer.

Let me summarize: Fifteen minutes of sex will not make your life, but it can ruin it. A lifetime of sex with the person you love is magical.

While sex has a climax with it, sex is not the climax of a relationship. Sex is akin to your pulse. The doc measures your pulse to indicate your health. Similarly, sex indicates something about you.

Don't try this while engaged in sex, but at an opportune moment, ask yourself about sex. Why? Why do I want this? What do I want from sex?

Don't settle for the answer, "Because it's fun." Of course it's fun. It's sex. But there's more to it than fun. Knowing that, examine it more closely—like a jeweler examines the facets of a diamond. That clarity will make sex great.

Otherwise, sex occludes—fogs, devalues, spoils—as in an inferior diamond.

Questions for Consideration

1. Sex doesn't make a relationship, it is an indicator about relationship. Agree or disagree and why? If you agree, and have this backwards, how do you correct your course?

2. We know why sex is fun, but what makes it magical?

3. Can sex hurt your soul, and if so, is there any such thing as safe sex?

CHAPTER 32

DISTINCT VERSUS SEPARATE[144]

If I say, "Your soul is *distinct* from your body," you appreciate an interesting point.

But if I *separate* your soul from your body, I have murdered you.

Prior to the Enlightenment (1685-1815), and specifically the philosophical thinking and writing of Immanuel Kant (1724-1804), the study of theology, mathematics, and the sciences overlapped. Each was a distinct subject, but there was integrated reliance and respect. Where one field excelled, the other capitalized on that expertise in order to facilitate its own field of study.

---

144 I have integrated into this chapter not only my own study, observation, and thought, but also the analysis from R.C. Sproul's, *The Consequences of Ideas*, referenced earlier, and Étienne Gilson's, *God and Philosophy*, also referenced earlier. I am indebted to both. I have also intentionally abridged the time frame and evolution of reason from Thomas Aquinas to Immanuel Kant in order to streamline *Swagger*. I believe the thinking behind this chapter, as well as the consequences of Kant's philosophy upon today's critical thinking, is accurate, but for a thorough critique, I recommend my sources to you.

Intellectual pursuits were distinct by subject, but not separate in that each was independent and self-reliant.

But with Kant, the sciences and theology diverged.

Within the sciences, anything that is known is known because it can be proven empirically. For Kant, empiricism meant anything provable by his five senses. Everything else, including self, ideas, and God, are perceptions and can't be fully known since they can't be empirically proven.

Sproul writes, "[Saint] Paul argued that, although God is 'invisible' or imperceivable, nevertheless he is 'seen' and 'known.' Paul declares not that God is seen directly through sense perception but that he is perceived in and through the created order."[145]

Paul is arguing the existence of God based upon perception of creation and the implication of created order. Kant is saying the existence of God can't be known because He can't be touched, tasted, heard, seen, or smelled—literally, empirically. Paul is arguing from two distinct realms—physical and mental—that work together to render truth. Kant is separating the two into empirical and nonempirical and concluding the existence of God can't be known.

Sproul again: "If Kant is correct in his critique, then Paul is wrong. Conversely, if Paul is correct in his assertions, then Kant is wrong. Both cannot be right."[146]

The purpose of this chapter is not to prove or disprove God. It is to make an observation: By adopting Kant's philosophy and eliminating the collaborative

---

145 Sproul, R.C. Ibid. Pp. 123-124. Cf. as well, Romans 1:18-23. NASB.

146 Ibid. P. 124.

approach to reason, our experience and exercise of reason today tends to be siloed, non-collaborative, separate, and self-contained as opposed to distinct but collaborative.

As an aside observation, we tried siloed thinking in business for a while and realized the foolishness of the approach, i.e. the bottom line suffered. However, society continues to keep science and theology separate, i.e. siloed.

You will encounter siloed thinking across life's spectrum. My observation is that folks utilize the distinct versus separate approach as suits their purpose. Unless you work in an empirical field doing empirical studies, maintaining separation tends to be inefficient and self-limiting.

Prior to Kant, Thomas Aquinas (1225-1274) referred to theology as the "queen of the sciences." His philosophical approach leveraged the strengths of each discipline of study from theology, to mathematics, to philosophy, etc. to acquire knowledge collaboratively. Aquinas' synthesis was his triumph and the culmination of sixteen hundred years of thought that began with Socrates (470-399 BC).

In what Sproul describes as an arbitrary decision, Kant dismissed sixteen centuries of integrated thinking and turned to empiricism as the only arbiter of what can be known for certain. He rejects reason because he can't demonstrate it to his senses. Kant knows reason must exist because there are ethics and civility and philosophy. But, he denies that he can know for certain.

Kant was a persuasive speaker and writer—perhaps the first empiricist to write in addition to speaking. The world adopted Kant's perspective. The queen of sciences was dethroned and science was coronated as king.

Today, theology is suspicious of science—in many circles an enemy—while science views theology as naïve, mystical, and inferior. The tension between the fields of thought drives both toward entrenchment and isolation, i.e. the silo effect mentioned earlier.

If you think about it, science sheds a lot of light on the Bible. Through the study of physiology and microbiology, the biblical passage declaring that you are fearfully and wonderfully made takes on incredible depth of meaning.[147] The famous picture taken by the Hubble space telescope showing approximately 10,000 galaxies in a small section of the constellation Fornax is awe-inspiring. The expanse of creation is beyond comprehension and science helps us grasp magnitude, complexity, and resulting awe.

But mention the scientific opinion that the earth is billions of years old, as opposed to the few thousand years some believe Scripture conveys, and you realize quickly that the complimentary, trusted working relationship between theology and science is a thing of the past. Assert that the universe was formed by the Big Bang, not creation as perceived in Genesis 1, and reconciliation of divergent perspectives becomes unlikely as the sides entrench within their silos of thought. Each is suspicious of the other.

---

147 Psalm 139:14. NASB.

This siloed thinking is not only evident in science and theology. It exists in many fields. For example, as I write, the medical industry is clamoring for more primary care physicians, i.e. family docs. For years, treatment protocols desired specialists—and as we have discovered, a specialty physician lacks the skills to integrate multi-faceted medical proficiency to ensure a healthy patient. As I write, the world is quarantined in an effort to manage the spread of the coronavirus, COVID-19, which has caused a worldwide pandemic. My neighbor, a neurologist, tells me she is seeing 40% of her normal volume of patients. Surgeons are not doing surgery. Because, all docs don't treat all diseases and maladies.[148]

Silos are good places to store grain. They are a poor concept where collaboration and integration are beneficial.

Theology, metaphysics, and philosophy specialize in the question of, why. Why am I here? Why are we here? Why is the universe here? And the answers are not because my parents conceived me, or so I can earn a living, or to participate in forming a society, or because the Big Bang happened. The question is seeking reason, significance, purpose, and the essence of meaning.

Science not only can't answer this question—it's not what science does—science has no structure to even pose the question. This is problematic. Bad things happen if you lose or can't establish meaning. Worse things occur if your disposition doesn't encourage or provide for you to seek outside counsel.

---

148 To read more about this professional dynamic, I refer you to my friend, Dr. Richard Young. *DrRichardAYoung.com*. <http://drrichardayoung.com/>. Accessed, 27 April 2020.

Science can tell us what and how, but why explains why something—humans, the universe, creation—matters. Creation has scientific significance for purposes of study, but why creation and humanity are here—i.e., have meaning, worth, value, being, essence—is a question only theology and philosophy can pose and answer.

Dr. Francis Collins is head of the National Institutes of Health, the government's hub for medical research. In his book, *The Language of God: A Scientist Presents Evidence for Belief*, Dr. Collins makes the case for a harmony between science and Christianity as he explores neuroscience and the brain. When asked about neuroscientific consciousness, he said,

> In terms of the scientific basis of consciousness, we really don't have a clue. In terms of the spiritual significance, obviously it's pretty important that we human beings seem to be special in our awareness of ourselves and our ability to imagine what other people are feeling at a given moment. All that is part of consciousness. I was an atheist when I entered medical school. I was a Christian when I left — and it was much driven by this experience of trying to integrate the reductionist aspects of science into the much more fundamental issues I saw my patients wrestling with, like is there a God and does God care about me and what happens after I die?
>
> Those are uncomfortable questions for an atheist 23-year-old, but ultimately they became totally compelling and required some investigation and some answers. Ultimately, out of that, it came to me that it makes a lot more sense to believe in God than to deny God's existence. A scientist isn't supposed to make assertions that you would call universal negatives, because you can never have enough evidence to do that, and yet that's what atheism calls you to do.
>
> I surprised myself as I began to look at the pros and cons of belief versus nonbelief — that actually through science there seem to be a fair number of pointers, not proofs, but pointers

toward the idea of a creator and a creator who was not only interested in creating something out of nothing, but also in having that something ultimately give rise to creatures with big brains who would have consciousness, who would have self-awareness, and who would have curiosity not just about nature, but also about who they are and what kind of spiritual creatures they might be.

It took me a couple of years to get through those many thickets of intellectual debate, but it led me then at that point in my life to see science and spirituality as not in conflict but actually quite compatible, quite harmonious, quite self- and co-reinforcing. People said my head was going to explode, that it would not be possible to both study genetics and read the Bible. I've never found a problem with this at all, despite the way in which some scientists have caricatured faith to make it seem incompatible. Most of those caricatures don't resemble my faith.

Similarly, the way that some people have caricatured science as a threat to God, that doesn't resemble the science that I'm doing. It's been a terrible, I think, consequence of our last century or so that this polarization has been accepted as inevitable when I see it not at all in that light. There are many interesting scientific questions that tap into the kind of area that you're asking about, like what is the neuroscientific basis of consciousness? What is the neuroscientific basis of a spiritual experience? If there is such a neuroscientific basis, does that make this spiritual experience less meaningful or more so?[149]

In sacrificing distinction to embrace separation, everyone loses. The Bible can't explain biology, but science can. Science can't account for why there is meaningful life, but theology can.

---

149 Reed, Jebediah. "A Long Talk with Anthony Fauci's Boss About the Pandemic, Vaccines, and Faith." July 1, 2020. *NYMag.com*. <https://nymag.com/intelligencer/2020/07/anthony-faucis-boss-on-why-things-could-be-much-better-soon.html>. Accessed, 4 July 2020.

Maintaining distinction as a field of study is fine, but to separate the studies leaves both bereft of what the other does and contributes. Worse yet, it requires each to study in areas where they lack expertise and make decisions for which they are ill-equipped.

Kant was highly influential. His philosophy was embraced, likely viewed as the pinnacle of enlightened thinking and the Enlightened Age. The separation of theology and science placed man decisively in charge of his own fate with every confidence he could figure it out. This was the birth of humanism, i.e. a belief in man and man as master of his fate.

Over two hundred years have passed since Kant. His influence remains, but let's take a cursory examination of history since Kant to see if it enlightens us regarding his philosophy and the embrace of separate at the expense of distinct.

The French Revolution of 1789 was the culmination of the high period of enlightened vision. There was a throwing out of old authorities, and this devolved into a bloody, tyrannical terror. The limit of enlightened thinking and revolutionary ideals was clear—and the outcome well recorded.

A decade later, Napoleon rose to power and Europe was gripped with war and conquest. Lord Wellington's diplomatic maneuvers following his victory over Napoleon at Waterloo staged Europe for the atrocities of World War I.

Our enlightened forefathers were not off to a very good start.

In the chapter, "Where Did God Go?," we conducted an overview of the tumultuous twentieth century: It was the bloodiest century in the history of mankind.

Not to be simplistic, but to make a cogent point, Kant's philosophy mentored Karl Marx, the father of Communism, a utopian ideal that saw the murder of multiplied millions deemed enemies of the [utopian] state. The logic of Kant's work was voiced eloquently and convincingly by Friedrich Nietzsche, wildly popular and read by thousands, the most prominent of whom was Adolf Hitler, mastermind of the Jewish genocide known as the Holocaust, and together with Joseph Stalin, instigator of World War II.

Trying to make sense of the tumultuous, brutal, nineteenth century, and the five decades of war to start the twentieth century, French philosopher Jean-Paul Sartre determined that man has no innate purpose. He utilized the philosophical logic of Immanuel Kant as the basis of his reasoning.

That's a pleasant thought. You are a thing—a simple thing—with no innate purpose.

While Kant was agnostic about God, Sartre declared his atheism, i.e. there is no God. Since there is no God, there can be no prior idea of human beings, no design or purpose for mankind, no essence. To make certain his hopeless point was delivered, Sartre wrote that man is not even created, he just exists.

There is no reason for anything, everything is contingent, all things share equal meaninglessness. To exist is simply to be present, an obscene, illegitimate presence. There are no rules, no norms to govern behavior. Freedom is freedom from morality, Sartre argued.[150] He must have been a delightful dinner guest.

One would think an enlightened world, filled with smart people, especially academic worlds populated by educated folks conversant in human history, would realize that separating theology from any or all of our pursuits renders bad outcomes. One would think smart people would recognize their mistake and turn to theology, metaphysics, and philosophy for insight.

But all of these were dismantled by empiricism and viewed as having little value. Inside a silo, you don't know what you don't know. One would think though.... But, not so.

Kant's arbitrary turn away from an integrated approach to reason— an integration where science, mathematics, theology, and philosophy collaborated and shared strengths and insights—in favor of the enlightened approach of scientific empiricism being the pinnacle of thought from which all other truths are derived, is now the standard for thought and analysis.

The philosopher R.C. Sproul calls this shift, Gilson's Choice, after the French philosopher, Étienne Gilson who identified the schism created by Kant. As you listen and learn, and hopefully think critically, you need to understand the basis of the logic and rationale now infecting every field of study.

As I write to you, America is terribly divided. We are no longer many distinct individuals who are Americans. We are many separated groups—

---

150 Heter, Storm. "Sartre's Political Philosophy." *Internet Encyclopedia of Philosophy* (IEP). <https://www.iep.utm.edu/sartre-p/>. Accessed, 27 April 2020.

what the pundits call hyphenated-Americans—who have lost our ability to collaborate. Our national motto, *E Pluribus Unum,* "out of many, one," is at grave risk. America has been referred to as "the great melting pot." Our language, culture, style, laws, and lands are an amalgamation of many into one.

I don't care whether you are a Democrat, Republican, Independent, or whatever else might form among political persuasions. What I care passionately about is that you engage with society and that you engage thoughtfully and respectfully.

The chapters in this small book are important aspects of how life in the West unfolds. Think. Examine. Read. Insist that courses of action make sense. I've written to you with ideas and perspectives to goad you into thinking, engaging, and living intentionally.

I hope you realize there is another vantage point from which to consider all things. Just because the world embraced Kant's separatism doesn't mean you have to. Return to Aquinas and his predecessors. Be shrewd. Understand. Don't swallow hook, line, and sinker what you are told. Learn to be wise.

This chapter does not propose to solve the pitfalls of distinction versus separation. It is meant to point it out so you see the impediment, examine it, and if convinced that it is as divisive as I hope to have demonstrated, then take steps to remedy what Kant led us into.

I am in the twilight of my years on Earth. While I remain, I will do all I can to help rectify our fundamental errors in reason in hopes society will come to its senses. If you are my age, I challenge you to be a voice of reason as well.

If you are younger, with your life before you, I encourage you to knock down the silos of separate thinking. As Bruce Cockburn said, "Kick at the darkness until it bleeds daylight."[151] Otherwise, you will live in a dark time for the philosophy of reason.

You will not survive separately. You must find yourself, sophisticate your distinctiveness, and then you and your colleagues must collaborate to integrate what you know, who you are, what can be known, and bring this to bear on what needs to be done. My counsel is that you adopt the philosophical position of Paul regarding the existence of God, not the arbitrary beliefs of Immanuel Kant.

United you stand. Divided you fall. Together you are greater than the sum of your parts. And for the record, God has gone to great lengths to be ready to join you.

E Pluribus Unum.

---

151 Cockburn, Bruce. "Lovers in a Dangerous Time." *Stealing Fire*. Spindrift Records. London, UK. 1984.

Questions for Consideration

1. Can you think of an example of siloed thinking? If so, what would it look like, and what would the benefit be potentially, of breaking down the silo of separateness?

2. What this chapter is asserting is that mankind might be less enlightened following the Age of Enlightenment than mankind was prior to enlightenment. Your thoughts?

3. Bruce Cockburn said, "Kick at the darkness until it bleeds daylight." What might this look like for you? What aspects of your life—and your world—are not as enlightened as you would like for them to be?

Chapter 33

WORTH

The most celebrated physicist of my day and recent times, the late Cambridge Professor Stephen Hawking, said, "The human race is just a chemical scum on a moderate-sized planet, orbiting around a very average star in the outer suburb of one among a hundred billion galaxies. We are so insignificant that I can't believe the whole universe exists for our benefit."[152]

As one bit of scum to another, surely there must be more value in us than Hawking stated.

Personal worth—human value, knowing you matter—is one of your essential needs as a human being. By essential, I mean you have to have personal worth—self-worth—in order to function optimally as a human.

---

152 Hawking, Stephen. *Goodreads.com* <https://www.goodreads.com/quotes/523470-the-human-race-is-just-a-chemical-scum-on-a>. Accessed, 28 April 2020.

Worth is like water. If you are thirsty, you will do anything to get a drink of water. If you are lacking self-worth, you will do anything to rectify your deficit.

One of my friends said, "When I put on my custom-tailored suit, I feel like a million dollars."

Another friend told me he bought his wife a new wedding ring. I asked if she lost the original. He said, "No, but she told me she felt inferior because Joyce had a bigger diamond than she did. We fixed that."

Years ago I was in New York City's East Village strolling through Tompkins Square Park. At the time, it was a hangout for people into the grunge fad. As the name implies, the more unkempt your appearance, the cooler you were considered to be. It was a hot day. Men and women alike were stripped down to their underwear—and less—so they could freely mark on each other's bodies with permanent markers—nothing artistic like a tattoo, rather any scribble to further deface their apparent worth to the world and thumb their nose at the world's worth to them.

As of July 17, 2020, at 5:00 PM Eastern, Jeff Bezos was worth $176 billion dollars.[153]

Churchill said, "We are all worms, but I do believe that I am a glow worm."[154]

---

153 Forbes. "#1 Jeff Bezos." *Forbes.com*. <https://www.forbes.com/profile/jeffbezos/# 1492d8fd1b23>. Accessed, 17 July 2020.

154 Churchill, Winston. Ibid.

In describing a colleague, a man told me, "He wears cheap shoes from a store in the mall, but he does a good job at work."

A friend who's done well financially says, "I wanted to be successful. I had to be successful. So, I climbed the ladder—and I got to the top. But the ladder was leaning against the wrong damn wall."

Self-worth.

Like air, you've got to have it. But how do you get it? If you are pond scum, or a worm, or almost naked in the park with marker all over you, what will it take to establish worth?

As I write, the COVID-19 pandemic is upon us and the world is quarantined to avoid the viral little pests. Last week, the price of oil dropped to negative $37. Oil millionaires yesterday are paupers today. If their self-worth was defined by oil, they are now worthless drags on society.

One of the most beautiful women of her day, Joan Collins, said, "The problem with beauty is that it's like being born rich and getting poorer."[155]

You can't buy enough, be enough, or be beautiful enough to secure sagging self-esteem. You can't earn it, or acquire it, nor can you ensure it.

I think Professor Hawking had two thoughts in his head simultaneously: one, the universe; the other, humanity. As a physicist, he measured Andromeda, took measure of mankind, and made his pronouncement: "We are so insignificant."

---

155 Collins, Joan. *BrainyQuote.com*. <https://www.brainyquote.com/quotes/joan_collins_103939>. Accessed, 28 April 2020.

On the one hand, the entire universe can't bestow self-worth upon you. On the other, compared to the stars, you are scum.

You lose either way.

Professor Hawking was an avowed atheist. He believed the universe is governed by the laws of science. "One can't prove that God doesn't exist. But science makes God unnecessary," he said. "No one created the universe and no one directs our fate."[156]

Like Professor Hawking, King David (c. 1035-970 BCE) was also a student of the stars. He too compared man to the heavens and pondered his self-worth. He wrote, "When I look at your heavens, the work of your fingers, / the moon and the stars, which you have set in place, / what is man that you are mindful of him, / and the son of man that you care for him?"[157]

David is wondering about his self-worth in light of his belief that God exists, notices him, and cares about him and his family.

Remove God from the universe and you are insignificant. Professor Hawking's assessment is accurate.

Establish God in the heavens and you matter. King David is correct.

---

156 Johnston, Lori. "'I'm not afraid': What Stephen Hawking said about God, his atheism and his own death." *WashingtonPost.com*. March 14, 2018. <https://www.washingtonpost.com/news/acts-of-faith/wp/2018/03/14/im-not-afraid-what-stephen-hawking-said-about-god-his-atheism-and-his-own-death/>. Accessed, 28 April 2020.

157 Psalm 8:3-4. ESV.

But this begs the question King David asked of God, "Why do you care about me?"

I don't know that you can answer the question of why God cares about you. But that doesn't invalidate the fact that He does.

> Could we with ink the ocean fill,
> And were the skies of parchment made;
> Were every stalk on earth a quill,
> And every man a scribe by trade;
> To write the love of God above
> Would drain the ocean dry;
> Nor could the scroll contain the whole,
> Though stretched from sky to sky.[158]

Why He loves, you don't know, but what it means to you, and what it tells you about yourself, can be understood—and adopted as true. The basic message of Christianity is that God redeemed you, even though irredeemable, through Jesus Christ's life, death, and resurrection to new life.

Here's an illustration of how this works:

Joe negotiates to buy a new-used truck for $20,000. He writes a check and slides it across the desk to the salesman—who in turn slides the truck keys to Joe. Their deal is sealed.

At this moment, the truck and the $20,000 are equivalent in worth. They are not equal. One is a truck and one is money, but in financial terms, they are equivalent in value.

---

158 Lehman, Frederick M. "The Love of God." 1917. Public Domain.

God comes to "purchase" a child. The cost is $JESUS.00. He determines that it's a good deal.

So, God pays $JESUS.00 to have you.

At this point, your worth—and Jesus' for that matter—is determined. Because of the price paid, worth is established: You and Jesus are equivalent in value. You are worth Jesus and Jesus is worth you.

This means that the next time you are diminished, devalued, demoralized; disenfranchised, discouraged, or otherwise considered less than, beneath, inferior, insignificant, or inadequate you have the legitimate right to attribute to yourself the worth that God declares is your true value.[159]

It's a stark comparison. God's absence or presence makes a substantive difference for you and your worth. Scum versus son or daughter of God.

Saint Matthew reports a story that Jesus told: "Again, the kingdom of heaven is like a merchant in search of fine pearls, who, on finding one pearl of great value, went and sold all that he had and bought it."[160] In order to help His listeners grasp a grand idea, Jesus uses a simile: "The kingdom of heaven is like…." He's saying, "In the kingdom of heaven, God behaves like a pearl merchant, who liquidates everything to possess one thing whose value is greater than everything."

---

159 Cf.: 1 Corinthians 6:20; 7:23. NASB.

160 Matthew 13:45-46. ESV.

This either made good economic sense to the pearl buyer or good sense as a beholder of beauty. That he sold everything means he knew exactly what he paid for the special pearl. Whatever he paid, that became the worth of that pearl.

God gave His everything—His only Son—to make it possible to have you.[161] Why this made sense to Him, you can't know. But that He did so establishes your worth.

Professor Hawking's atheism leaves no alternative but to determine your value based upon physics, natural laws, and his demeaning evaluation. Compared to the Pleiades, you are pond scum.

If God is, He loves you. That means you matter a great deal. Philosophically stated, you have existential significance. He placed the Pleiades in the heavens because He had you in mind and it pleased Him to affirm your worth.

Can this be replicated to satisfy the scientific standard? Not a chance.

But God's presence, care, and love—the mindfulness of God, the thing King David observed—can be known. Aquinas proved it—five different ways.[162] Pascal said you could sense it in your soul.[163] St. Paul taught that you live, and move, and have your being in God and that this can be perceived in the created order.[164]

---

161 John 3:16. NASB.

162 Cf.: Footnote 50 in *Swagger*.

163 Pascal, Blaise. *GoodReads.com*. <https://www.goodreads.com/quotes/801132-there-is-a-god-shaped-vacuum-in-the-heart-of-each>. Accessed, 30 April 2020.

164 Acts 17:28; Romans 1:18-20. NASB.

The need for worth. Significance. Personal value. You have options and two approaches.

Upon what basis will you establish your self-worth?

Questions for Consideration

1. The premise of this chapter is that self-worth is essential to your well-being—meaning you must have it. Your thoughts on this?

2. You are worth Jesus and Jesus is worth you. Is this an inspirational notion or literally true?

3. Preston writes that you have existential significance. What does this mean? Contrast that with Hawking's view of you. Which will you adopt, why, and upon what basis?

Chapter 34

THE MEDIA

The media is called the fourth estate.

In Europe, this refers to the media sharing power with the clergy, the nobility, and the commoners. In the United States, the fourth estate means the media is the fourth balance of power in conjunction with the three branches of government: the judiciary, the executive, and the legislative.

There is balance of power because those wiser than us recognized that power corrupts and absolute power corrupts absolutely.[165] While the various powers constantly angle for more power, American society treasures a free media and benefits when power is balanced.

Lots of places in the world communicate with their people via state-run media.

---

165 Acton Institute. Ibid.

Over the course of my days, I've traveled to a number of countries where the media is not free. They are given their stories by the governmental gods controlling them. If they fail to deliver the party line, bad things happen to them.

In America, our free media is a blessing, but blessed as we may be, it is to our advantage to understand what the media does.

Whatever else the media may be, it is a business that succeeds or fails based upon market share. The more of the market a media outlet controls, the more advertising dollars they command.

A few decades ago, there were only a few media outlets. Each enjoyed significant market share. Today, there are thousands of outlets scrambling to gain and hold enough market share to stay in business. It is impossible for an outlet to be all things to all people, so they must define themselves by the piece of the market they control.

Bluntly, this means their reporting is biased toward their market. The notion of an unbiased media is impossible. Think of it as customer satisfaction.

The media present us with stories. It's also called reporting. Either way, the media presents us with narratives about our world that keep us informed.

Every day, often multiple times per day, the media has to have a story. No story, no market share for that media outlet, and that means no funding, no revenue stream, no cash flow.

If there is no story, a story has to be found. Reporters hustle every day to find a story—just like you and your contemporaries must hustle every day to keep ahead, and just like your parents before you, and their parents before them hustled each day to make ends meet. It's the way the world works.

To have a story worth telling, there must be conflict. No conflict, no story— at least not a compelling story, and the media only tells compelling stories. You can't make a drawing without shadows.

So, every day the media has to have two things: 1) stories, 2) with conflict in them.

The better the story, i.e. the greater the conflict and consumer response, the more beneficial the story is to the media. The stronger or better the story, the more market share, and the more money from ad dollars.

But the markets, i.e. the consumers of media, don't want stories they don't want to hear or that confront them with misunderstanding or wrongheadedness. If you are a Republican, you don't want to hear how great the Democrats are. If you are pro-abortion, you don't want to read a story about when fetal heartbeats can be discerned.

In short, the media has biases. They position themselves as relaying the truth to you, but it's truth through a filter you and the media have chosen.

I have friends who listen exclusively to Fox News. I have friends who swear by CNN. I have friends who think *The New York Times* has the market cornered on truth.

When you read a news feed—about anything—appreciate the media folks delivering it to you. They are hustling. But understand what you're reading.

Bottom line: There is no such thing as an unbiased media or unspun story. Read accordingly.

And one more thing: Reading or listening to only what you want to hear, or to people who believe like you do, makes you intellectually inbred, not thoughtful, astute, and wise. Consider widely and wisely.

Questions for Consideration

1. A good story must have conflict in it to be a good story. Agree or disagree, and whichever persuasion you have, what's an example?

2. How should you go about getting the news? How should you evaluate what you hear? By what standard?

3. What are your core values in the primary arenas of your life? How do you stay informed? Are you interested in staying informed, interested in what the other side is saying, and is it necessary for you to stay broadly informed?

CHAPTER 35

OLD PEOPLE AND IDEAS

On May 22, 1982, the minister's voice boomed, "I now pronounce you husband and wife." I kissed Becky and we walked up the aisle arm-in-arm into our new life together.

After our honeymoon, she returned to her college studies in nursing while I continued my already thriving profession on the Christian speaking circuit. I was in and out of every Christian denomination you can name, more youth camps than you can count, and on more platforms speaking about spirituality than you can inventory. A book was in the works, my calendar was full, and the phone was ringing. Becky and I were happy, our lives full, and filled with promise.

On May 22, 1987, Becky graduated with her Bachelor of Science degree in Nursing. It was our fifth wedding anniversary, and that evening, after a celebratory dinner with our families, she said, "Preston, I don't want to live with you any longer. I want a divorce."

She gave no explanation, no reason, and no warning—even in retrospect. It remains one of my life's mysteries.

But leave she did, breaking my heart, taking most of our household goods with her, destroying my reputation, ruining me professionally, and compromising me financially. My calendar went from full to cancelled. I went from 150 pounds to 121. I wandered the woods until late in the night almost every night, often bloody from barbed wire fences and trees I clung to for solace until my face bled. I cooked with camp pots and owned one spoon. The months I spent homeless, living in my car during college, were not as destitute as the days following Becky's abandonment of us, her and me and the dog. Yes, even the dog suffered. Thank God there were no children.

In time, I healed. I emerged an entirely different man than the man who married Becky. Some years later I met Dianne. A few years after that, she said yes, and that was three decades ago.

No church, or youth group, or spiritual conference wants to hear from you after you are divorced. So, I had to reinvent myself professionally.

It's a long story, but I became the business mind behind a nonprofit, Christian ministry. The problem was, I knew nothing about business, especially the cut-throat, lawless business of the Christian not-for-profit world.

We had just finished building our new office space when an older friend asked if I would sublet office space to him. Carroll Ray[166] had been Chief of Internal Auditing for the Tandy Corporation. He'd taken early retirement only to discover he didn't like being retired early and was going back into business with a partner.

Not long after Carroll moved in with us, I was in my office laboring over a bookkeeping mystery. As I sat staring at the numbers, it dawned on me: *Carroll knows accounting and he's on the other side of my wall.*

Carroll's gone now, a victim of Parkinson's disease. He not only helped resolve my accounting mystery that day, but he took me under his wing. He became one of my business mentors. He taught me accounting, contracts, negotiation, personnel, tactics, and management. He introduced me to my other business mentor, Peter Drucker,[167] who's also gone from this life. Together, they taught me to think, taught me how to use my talents, taught me to integrate faith and practice, and taught me how to select the right kinds of people as advisors. They told me stories of their time in business. Vicariously, I mirrored their strategies to establish my own precedents and style. I still hear their voices in my head.

By the time Carroll retired the second time, we were close friends and colleagues, one old, one younger. We ate lunch together often. On any number of occasions, I moved my chair next to his and laid a page between

---

166 Ray Jr., Carroll B. *Legacy.com*. February 22, 2007. <https://www.legacy.com/obituaries/name/carroll-ray-obituary?pid=178189430>. Accessed, 29 April 2020.

167 Drucker, Peter. "Peter Drucker." *Wikipedia.org*. <https://en.wikipedia.org/wiki/Peter_Drucker>. Accessed, 29 April 2020.

us for consideration and counsel. We read books together, critiqued them, adopted the best ideas, and capitalized on the genius of others. Carroll and Mr. Drucker showed me how to be humble, observe, learn from others, and ultimately, how to lead and guide others. Together, they helped me become comfortable with my latent talent for business and nonprofit business.

I'm indebted to these two men who came before me, shared their lives with me, and left substantive portions of themselves inside my soul. Because they invested in me, I'm able to invest in others. Because they were transparent with their lives and experiences, I'm inspired to follow their example. The current term for this is "paying it forward." What they did for me was called mentoring.

Not all old people are suitable mentors. Not all old people are worthwhile counselors, but many are. I'm sharing part of my story in hopes it inspires you to access the lifetime of experience in the older people around you.

To be certain, many will not be helpful, even if they want to assist you. But others? Oh, my. Others can form practices and perspectives in you that you would never apprehend in a lifetime on your own.

Take advantage of these people. Follow my lead with Carroll. I humbled myself, risked his rejection, picked up my deficiencies, and asked for his assistance. Most old people are glad to assist. They've lived a lifetime. The wise ones know they can't take life with them so are happy to give it to a younger person who recognizes their historic value.

By the time a person is old, they've figured out that life has more questions than it does answers. They know about resilience and they have a grip on what matters. Best of all, they aren't your parents, so their only vested interest in you is appreciation that a younger human respects them as an older human.

Life is hard enough as it is. Life's really hard if you start from scratch.

My mentors are dead now, but they both taught me to seek counsel. Over the years, I've maintained what I call my personal board of counsel. This is a stable of 4-7 folks—men and women—who I visit with on a regular basis. Each is a person whose voice I listen to. Not many are older than I am in years, but they are all old people in that they are savvy about life. Each is old in that they have observed me and known me long enough to understand me.

The person who fails to access the wealth of wisdom embodied in the old people around them is a poor person. They are destined to learn inefficiently via the school of hard knocks.

My counsel?

Don't be that person. Instead, access old people. Most will generously invest themselves into you if you ask.

If you approach an older person and it isn't right, or they can't help, what have you lost? A cup of coffee perhaps?

But if you approach an elder and discover a gold mine, like I did with my mentors? Well, you've found a treasure.

Questions for Consideration

1. *What might the composition of your board of advisors look like? Who would you place on this board? How would you access them, with what frequency, and for what occasions?*

2. *How old must a book be in order to be authoritative? A person? A concept?*

3. *What's required to seek personal counsel? Humility? Courage? Crisis? Confidence?*

Chapter 36

WHO ARE YOU?

We used to say, he's a doctor, a lawyer, an Indian chief. I suppose now we should reference a health care professional, a doctor of jurisprudence, or a Native-American tribal official.

Here's the deal: However you spin the terms, by whatever name, all the answers are wrong.

You are not what you do.

You can't be, you mustn't be. Otherwise, when you retire or lose your job you are nothing. If you are what you do and you screw up, then you are a screw up. If you fail, then you are a failure. If you lose, then you are a loser. If you are rejected, then you are a reject. If the market crashes, then you are worthless.

If your performance defines who you are, then your identity is constantly in flux. This is not sustainable, but this is the norm for how we think about and identify ourselves. Consequently, the entire world is devoted to performance-based identity, an unreachable, unsatisfactory, unsustainable, misguided goal.

Who you are—your person—must be distinguished from your performance. While the world around you twists and spins to establish an elusive identity based upon societal norms that are undefined and in flux, you don't have to play the game.

You have an alternative.

But what if you are the product of what someone else did?

If you are an illegitimate child, then you are a bastard. If you are assaulted, you are dirty. If you don't have as much as someone else, you are disenfranchised. If you are born brown, you are a minority, and if you are born black the question is whether you are black enough? If you are born white, you are privileged—whether you think you are or not. Red? You are a victim.

If you embrace that you are defined by what someone else did, or by how many of you there are in a population, or by the color of your skin, then you are fighting an irrevocable stigma, a pointless battle, and a misguided ideal that will render you heartache and dissatisfaction.

You also have an alternative.

The world will always define you down over something. God always lifts you up.

The message of the Bible is that if you are a disciple—a follower—of Jesus Christ, a Christian, then this world is not your true home, you're just passing through. The message of the Bible is that your family of origin is not your true family. You are a child of God. The message of the Bible is that what you do, or what's done to you, does not define you.

God declares who you are and what's true about you because you belong to Him. Your performance and appearance are important to Him, but they have ZERO to do with your true identity.

Living from the basis of a secure identity, you are free to perform. The undue burden of a performance-based acceptance is removed. It's a great alternative to the alternative.

Here's how He remade you and redefined you: The message of the Bible is that God considered everything wrong with you, classed all of it into one term, sin—i.e. literally, shortfall—and paid the consequence of sin, one time, in full, in perpetuity, through Jesus Christ.

Saint Paul wrote, "I am crucified with Christ,"[168] which begs the question: Since I'm alive and well, what part of me died when Jesus died on the cross?

There are books and more books on this subject,[169] but for our purposes, your old identity died. In its place, God declared a new identity is true of you.[170]

You're not a doctor, or a lawyer, or a potentate. You're not a frat guy, a cheerleader, or a ball player. Nor are you a banker, waitress, dad or mom,

---

168 Galatians 2:20. NASB.

169 Consider the suggested reading list in the back of *Swagger* and the brief descriptions of each.

170 The theological basis for this is Romans 5:12-8:39. I recommend you read from either the NASB or ESV.

business owner or employee. You're not a screw-up or a failure. You're not a bastard, SOB, victim, minor player in society, and neither are you red, yellow, black, white, or brown. You're not rejected, flawed, worthless, unloved, alone, dismissed, or disenfranchised. You are not a hyphenated anything. Neither are you defined by your intelligence, accolades, talents, achievements, beauty, the clothes on your back, or your net worth. Whether you drive a Mercedes, ride the bus, or get around town on a bicycle has no bearing on who you are. In fact, God doesn't even think of you as male or female.[171]

If you are a follower of Jesus Christ, you belong to God. You are loved, accepted, and part of a forever family; you are included, indwelt by God; redeemed, forgiven, and set apart as special to God; in Him you are competent, secure, safe, courageous, and formed by God Himself.[172]

From this perspective, the question isn't who you are. Your identity is determined, declared, and decided with finality by God because you are His child.

Practically speaking, you will perform within your concept of yourself.

If your self-identity fluctuates based upon what others do or say, and what you perceive and do, then your self-concept will stay in flux. In turn, this will affect your performance, i.e. thought, emotion, and behavior.

---

171 Galatians 3:28. NASB.

172 Cf.: 1 Corinthians 6:20; 7:23; John 3:16; Galatians 4:7; Ephesians 1:7; Romans 3:24; 15:7; Ephesians 1:10 and 11; 2:13; 2:19; 3:6; 5:30; Galatians 3:29; 1 Corinthians 3:16; 6:19; 2 Timothy 1:14; Romans 8:11; John 16:13; Ephesians 1:7; Colossians 1:14; Hebrews 9:15; Ephesians 1:7; 4:32; Colossians 1:14; 2:13; Hebrews 10:18; Colossians 1:2; 6:11; Hebrews 2:11; 10:10; Philippians 4:13; Hebrews 4:15; Romans 8:38-39; 2 Corinthians 10:17; Ephesians 3:12; Philippians 1:6; Titus 3:8; Hebrews 13:6; Acts 17:28; Psalm 22:10; 139:13; Galatians 1:15. NASB.

If you base your self-concept on what was done to you, this will define self-concept and be a predictor of your performance. Typically, either pity or passion.

If you identify as a victim, you will behave as such and believe yourself disenfranchised. Disrespect will be the theme of your life.

Identify as an overcomer, you will achieve. This is good and people will love you for what you produce—today. Tomorrow is a new day and yesterday no longer matters.

Others-based acceptance and performance-based acceptance. Your self-concept is only as stable as what your sense of self is based upon and your ability to perform in that arena. Get hustling.

The message of Christianity is that when you become a follower of Jesus Christ, God declares an identity of you that is true all the time, that does not waver under any circumstance, and that is founded upon a declaration by God, no one else, and nothing else.

In practice, this means your self-concept is determined, declared, and static, i.e. secure, unchanging, unwavering, and sure. Within this self-concept you are now free to perform to your human potential unimpeded by a self-concept subject to whim, outside opinions or forces, or the pressure of having to perform or achieve in order to remain viable as a person.

You are free to build your identity as suits you. What will you select as your basis?

Questions for Consideration

1. You've heard it said that you can be anything you want to be. True or false and what's your reasoning?

2. What impact should failure have upon your self-worth? What impact should success have on your self-worth?

3. What have you decided to base your identity upon? Others and their feedback? Yourself and your wherewithal? What God says?

CHAPTER 37

MY VIEW OF YOU

Generations used to be identified by family names. Here's some of what I heard growing up:

"Pop (my paternal grandfather) was given extra government coupons during the war (WWII) so he could buy tires for our old car. All the rubber was going toward the war effort. But as a minister (Presbyterian), the government knew he needed to visit grieving parishioners who had lost loved ones."

"Your great, great grandmother, Susan, was a Cherokee Indian who met your great, great grandfather, an Irish immigrant, on the Trail of Tears (1838-1840). She buried two babies along the trail."

"Granddaddy (maternal grandfather) was the fire chief and postmaster during the war. He was too young for the first war and too old for the second (i.e. WWII). He was embarrassed his whole life that he hadn't served."

After World War II, sociologists began identifying generations by generational names. Tom Brokaw coined the WWII generation, the Greatest Generation.[173] Chuck Underwood, a generational expert, called them the Silent Generation,[174] for good reason. Their children, of whom I'm one, were labeled Baby Boomers. Our kids, Generation X. Theirs, Millennials. Followed by Gen Z, and so on.

I have no quibbles with Chuck Underwood, whom I've met two or three times, or Mr. Brokaw, whom I don't know, but who is a fly fisherman and thus must be a fine person. They have been strong contributors to our social understanding. My observation is that regardless of the events that catalyze to form a generation, all human beings are formed from the same building blocks.

My psychology studies debated nurture versus nature: Are babies born with inherent qualities, e.g. personality or talents or abilities, or are they born a blank slate, what Aristotle and John Locke termed, *tabula rasa?*[175]

I believe you, like every other baby, were formed fearfully and wonderfully within your mother's womb, just as the Book of Psalms states.[176] This includes some known qualities and some qualities that became evident after you exited your mom and made your presence known.

---

173 Kagan, Julia. "The Greatest Generation." *Investopedia.com*. Updated April 13, 2020. <https://www.investopedia.com/terms/t/the_greatest_generation.asp>. Accessed, 30 April 2020.

174 Underwood, Chuck. *The Generational Imperative*. BookSurge. North Charleston, SC. P. 40ff.

175 Encyclopedia Britannica. "Tabula Rasa." *Britannica.com*. <https://www.britannica.com/topic/tabula-rasa>. Accessed, 30 April 2020.

176 Psalm 139:14. NASB.

Granted, you were malleable, like a lump of clay on the potter's wheel, but you had presence. You had essence, existence, and a future. Regardless of whether you were planned or a surprise, wanted or unwanted, God formed you because He has intent for your existence and your future. I believe this is true for every human being.

Our fundamental building blocks are the same. Maslow[177] and others identified them. They are the essentials, the basic needs shared by all human beings, including: acceptance, love, belonging, worth, significance, competency. You must have these needs supplied, just like you must have food, water, and shelter.

As Maslow and others observed, if one of these essentials is unmet, other things are left wanting until you can satisfy your unmet essential. In my line of work as a therapist, my clients all had unmet needs. It was as though they carried life's water in a leaky bucket. Once life got demanding enough, they couldn't put water into the bucket of life fast enough. In desperation, they came to me empty, frustrated, and demoralized looking for assistance.

There are enough building blocks, assembled with enough variables—family, culture, genetics—filtered through your God-given personality, and tailored with your experiences to create a human being unlike any other human in the history of humanity. At your core, you are like everyone else. In your complex state as the current you, you are totally unique. No one else has your fingerprint, the pattern of your iris, or your temperament amalgamation. Neither does anyone else have your manner, your face, or your ingenuity.

---

177 Cherry, Kendra. "The 5 Levels of Maslow's Hierarchy of Needs." *VeryWellMind.com*. December 3, 2019. <https://www.verywellmind.com/what-is-maslows-hierarchy-of-needs-4136760>. Accessed, 6 May 2020.

At the highest level of this concept, you are the only you there will ever be. If you squander you, you rob the rest of us—even afflict us. If you leverage you, you make the rest of us greater.

Each day, you have one, basic decision to make as soon as your eyes open: Will I live my best today?

An aspect of this book has been to offer thoughts about how to live your best life. Beginning now. I've offered you opinions and perspectives—thoughts I wish I had known sooner. Of course, what you do with these chapters and your life is your decision. But at least you hold a few more cards in your hand now than you did when you first picked up this book.

As illustrated in these pages, our forefathers made mistakes. They aborted God and adopted humanism. They became arrogant and separated themselves into silos. They accumulated, thinking they would acquire happiness, only to be burdened.

Those before us also made wise decisions. They turned their lives over to One greater, One pledged to meet all their essential needs. They entered the arena. They failed, and succeeded, and some died trying. They laid their lives down so others could pick theirs up.

Together, we form the human race, not to compete against each other, but to collaborate in being our best. Distinct, not separate. Determined, not blaming. Composed. Thoughtful. At peace with the end in mind. Anchored with inescapable truths, not adrift in the sea of relativism. Fulfilled because we've seized God's outstretched hand and are secure, filled with His presence, and part of something larger than self.

At a spiritual level, we all have what Pascal called "the God-shaped vacuum."[178] No matter what is put into that vacuum, anything but God will be sucked up and you will be left wanting, lugging a leaky bucket through life. But with God's initiative, a new bucket is yours to appropriate. If you do this—accept God's proposal of life in Him through Jesus Christ—then you bring to all around you an expression of God that only you can communicate and demonstrate.

Within your soul—the thinking, feeling, choosing capacities—you are profound. This is the fundamental you, your person, and if you bring yourself to the rest of us, together we become greater than the sum of our parts. But bring us all of you, otherwise you are an impediment and a mystery that saps you and us.

Your earthly suit, your physical self, the temporary part of you that will pass away in your lifetime: It's a wonderful creation, uniquely designed to convey the unique you to us. It smiles, cries, touches, holds, and is warm and alive. We've learned over time that a human who is not touched does not thrive—touched literally and touched figuratively. Make this expressive vehicle—your physical self—compellingly present to us so that we benefit from you. Be present and accounted for.

All of this to say, regardless of your generational title, I believe in you. I believe you have the self-awareness—if you will pay attention—to sense God moving midst your essential needs.[179] I believe you have the ability to love

---

178 Pascal, Blaise. Ibid.

179 Philippians 4:19. NASB.

yourself and others. I believe you can contribute, not that you haven't already, but in the coming days to contribute beyond your wildest imagination.

I believe you have the ability to reach out and touch the face of God.

Now, go into the world. Love God. Be at peace. Love and serve all mankind. And when you reach your final day, may you have played all the music that was in you to play.

Questions for Consideration

1. If you are you, and no one else is, what is your responsibility to the rest of us?

2. What does it mean to you that God made you fearfully and wonderfully? What bearing does this have on how you live life and conduct yourself?

3. The last paragraph is Preston's blessing and charge to you. Please take some time to consider how each aspect inspires, and affects, and enlightens how you live. Now, what does that look like?

CHAPTER 38

WHO I AM

I am the descendant of immigrants, scoundrels, patriots, ministers, and courageous individuals. All that made them runs in my veins.

I discovered America in Wilson, Oklahoma during a snowstorm. I am the oldest of four, all brothers. Mason and Wade are dead. Will and I remain, two of four.

From Wilson, my family moved to Okmulgee, then to Edmond, then to Stillwater, and then to Durant. We were poor. My clothes were used, but I didn't think much about it.

I started earning my own way when I was ten, in the fifth grade. Since then, I've never not had a job—or two. Work is good.

My grandparents, uncles and aunts, cousin, brothers, and parents are buried in the red dirt of Poteau, Oklahoma. That's where my maternal grandfather, Marcus, was born while Oklahoma was Indian Territory, not yet a state.

I began college at Southeastern Oklahoma State University. I declared a major in psychology but discovered history.

As a junior, I transferred to Missouri State University. My psychology classes transferred but didn't amount to a degree plan, so I declared history my new major and that was providential. I learned to read, and write, and research, and think.

I put myself through college and grad school. I was homeless for a while—living out of my car, making meals on my camp stove, and cleaning up as I could. I worked multiple jobs, let my white-blond hair grow, and focused on getting through school.

In time, I rented a room. In grad school, I rented a basement room with a shared shower. I cut wood, and did this and that, and endeavored to eat one decent meal a day.

When I landed a janitorial job, I made enough money to rent an apartment with a small balcony. I sat there most evenings.

I was a runner in those days. Across the street from my apartment was a national cemetery with a wall between the Union dead and the Confederate dead. It was quiet there—and I ran. A lot.

In 1978, I graduated with my degree in history—ancient history, or antiquities. After some starts and stops, I walked the stage for the last time in 1981 with a graduate degree in Guidance and Counseling.

My university days were significant in forming and forging me into the man I am. Degrees in the liberal arts leave a lot more room for professional creativity. Said another way, no one was looking for me when I graduated. I made up my career, which was okay by me. But my life-long boss (me) can be a hard man to work for some days.

In education and then in private practice, I'm a therapist who learned far more about humanity studying history than he did studying human behavior. From grappling with the concerns of individuals, I moved into business and began grasping what it took to manage and guide a group of people. In time, I worked with larger groups, more diverse groups, and even countries of people. I have traveled and worked all over North America, the Caribbean, Europe, western Asia, and parts of the Middle East.

These days, I spend most of my time writing—primarily fiction. But when an interesting opportunity presents itself to guide an organization and its leaders in strategic initiatives, leadership development, or transitions, I'll participate.

My knees won't run anymore, but I ride a bicycle to stay in shape and be able to fly fish. I use a stick these days to navigate the currents and rocks, and as Norman Maclean wrote, when I'm fly fishing "…all existence fades to a being of my soul and memories and the sounds of the… river and a four-count rhythm and the hope that a fish will rise."[180]

---

180 Maclean, Norman. *A River Runs Through It and Other Stories*. University of Chicago Press. Chicago, IL. 1976. P. 104.

I'm married to Dianne, an absolutely lovely woman. She has spent over thirty years teaching in Title One (underprivileged) schools, grades Pre-Kindergarten (age 4), Kindergarten, and First Grade. We have twins, Alex and Anna. They both live in heaven.

I'm the chief grocery shopper, cook, and house manager. Most nights, I'm at the grill, under the Live Oak tree. My compatriot is Braxie-the-dog, a Basenji,[181] the barkless breed, known as the dog of the Pharaohs. Braxie weighs twenty pounds and her breed was used to hunt lions. She's hard-headed, not unlike her master.

I was born and raised in Oklahoma, studied in Missouri, and moved to Fort Worth, Texas in 1982. Steinbeck coined the term, Okie, in *Grapes of Wrath*.[182] It was meant as pejorative—disapproval of those from Oklahoma. But we Okie's made it ours. Texas is home, but the red dirt of Oklahoma formed my bones.

If you want to know even more about who I am, I refer you to:

PrestonGillham.com.[183]

From the bottom of my heart, thank you for reading my book. I'm honored. To enter your world, speak into your soul, and offer thoughts is a respect you have granted and one that I treasure.

---

181 American Kennel Club. "Basenji." *AKC.org*. <https://www.akc.org/dog-breeds/basenji/>. Accessed, 30 April 2020.

182 Steinbeck, John. *The Grapes of Wrath*. Penguin Classic. New York, NY. 1936, 2006.

183 Gillham, Preston. *PrestonGillham.com*. <http://www.prestongillham.com/>. Accessed, 30 April 2020.

APPENDIX A

How to Become a Christian

The key to any relationship, even a relationship with God, is mutual respect. While I could write pages and pages on mutual respect and relationships, the point of this appendix is to consider relationship with God, i.e. becoming a Christian, a follower of Jesus Christ, a disciple of His, or simply, a Believer.

When God made you, He endowed you with an independent, free will. Certainly, God will be persuasive, as any strong individual will be with their perspective, but out of respect for your self-determination, He will not force Himself upon you. If you and He are going to have a relationship, it will only be because you both agree of your own volition to enter into relationship.

In this book, I've likened this to marriage. It's an apt parallel. Both must agree and say "I do" to have a marriage.

God went to great lengths to make relationship possible. He did this by taking on humanity and coming to live among humankind. We know this event as Christmas, or the Incarnation, and recognize the person as Jesus Christ.

God took it upon Himself—as and through Jesus Christ—to remove all impediments that would preclude you and Him from enjoying a viable, vibrant, and vital relationship. All that was wrong, He made right. All that could go wrong, He made provision for. All of this, He accomplished in and through Jesus Christ.

The Bible verbalizes it like this: In your independence, you fall short of God's standard, i.e. you sin. In your humanity, you are flawed as the descendant of a flawed progenitor and race.[184] Said another way, you fall short and sin, and by nature, you are a sinner.

Two problems stand between you and God, and a relationship: a) your sinful performance and b) your identity as a sinner.

So, becoming a Christian and being accepted by God is not simply being forgiven for the things you do wrong. You also need to be remade. Jesus said it like this: You need a new Father, a new life. You have to be born again in order to be part of a new family.[185]

Through Jesus Christ, God made provision for your poor performance (sins, in biblical parlance). Through Jesus Christ, God does away with your old

---

184 Romans 3:23; 5:12-21. NASB.

185 John 3:1-8. NASB.

identity (sin, the Bible calls it) and promises you a new identity as His child, i.e. forgiveness for what you've done and who you are.

There is only one thing standing between you and God. The one thing is you, or more specifically, your independent choice to accept His offer or remain a free agent. Recall my conversations with my atheist neighbor: He chose unfaith. I chose faith. Both of us made choices regarding how we would approach life and eternity.

The mutual respect aspect of this relationship looks like this: God will not violate your freedom of choice, but He will make a provision to remove everything standing between you and Him. Your part is: a) agreeing with Him about needing Him, and b) asking that He enter your life, forgive you of your sins and sinfulness, and give you new life.[186]

It's that simple.

To be clear though: Before becoming a Christian, you should make certain you understand that you are not simply buying a life insurance policy that ensures you go to heaven when you die and have your sins forgiven in this life. That's shortsighted. More than that, it's disrespectful, thereby calling into question your motive in the first place.

A relationship that is mutually respectful is a relationship committed to daily life together (more about this in a moment). If God simply wanted you in heaven, He would make it so. But He desires more than to populate heaven. He desires a relationship.

---

186 Cf.: John 1:12; Romans 10:8-10; Acts 16:31 (vss. 22-34). NASB.

The question is, do you as well?

If so, here's your next step: Discussing things with God is called prayer. Here's a simple statement you can make to God (in prayer). I promise you that He will hear your prayer, take you at your word, set things right between the two of you, and make you part of His family:

Lord God, thank you for hearing me as I pray. I'm coming to begin a relationship with you—the relationship you so generously offer. I've lived independently of you until now. But now, I relinquish being in charge of my own life and humbly ask you to forgive me where I've failed you and others. Would you make me your child, part of your eternal family? Would you make me a new person and begin your work in my life? I ask that you take charge and sit on the throne of my life. I recognize you as my Lord and God. I want you to live in me and I want to live in and through you. Thank you, Amen.

WHAT NOW?

Here are some suggested next steps designed to help you mature in the relationship you've begun with God.

As I mentioned in the chapter, "The Bible," I suggest you purchase one of the Bible versions referenced in the chapter and begin reading the Gospel of John. You can locate it in the Table of Contents in your Bible. It does a great job of introducing you to Jesus Christ. Once read, I recommend you read the Book of Ephesians next. It does a great job of introducing you to the new you.

I urge you to make reading a selection from the Bible a regular feature of each day. It would be best if you stayed in the New Testament until you get your spiritual feet underneath you. If you would like guidance on what to read each day, I refer you to YouVersion.com and their daily reading plan.

In addition to the Bible, I recommend you read *Lifetime Guarantee* by Bill Gillham. It will help you understand more about the spiritual transaction between you and God, what that means for your new identity, and offer practical applications that I believe will be advantageous to you.

To grasp more of God's perspective on His relationship with you, I suggest you read Malcolm Smith's book, *The Power of the Blood Covenant*. Your takeaway will be how serious God is about never releasing His grip on you.

Both Malcolm and Bill have audio resources that you can search and access.

If you've enjoyed this book and would like to subscribe, I write a blog. You can subscribe at PrestonGillham.com.

A place where you can meet other Believers is vital to your spiritual growth. Finding an appropriate church is important. I say "appropriate" because all churches are not equal. Locating a church is sort of like finding a new friend. Not all available are suitable, but many can be. Similarly, if you attend a prospective church and it just doesn't feel right, try another.

Churches come in a liberal variety and conservative variety. This is not liberal versus conservative like in politics, but liberal versus conservative in the way they view the Bible and Christianity.

Liberal churches and denominations have departed a conservative approach to Christianity and the Bible and adopted a socially liberal view instead. It will be difficult for you to grow in your Christian faith in one of these churches for the simple reason that they don't talk about the Bible, faith in Christ, and spiritual growth as much as they talk about social initiatives. While it's not possible to be categorical, Methodist, Disciples of Christ (also called Christian), Episcopal, and many Presbyterian churches are liberal leaning.

On the conservative side of things, churches called Bible churches, e.g. "XYZ" Bible Church, most Baptist, and some Presbyterian churches are conservative leaning. These are likely a good choice for you to look into because you will hear messages, and have access to programs, that will help you grow in your faith and be confident in your walk with Christ.

While this sounds overwhelming, the litmus test is simple and reliable: Does the church view the Bible—all of it—as the inspired, infallible Word of God? If so, you're good to go. If they flinch when you ask this question, keep looking.

If Bible Study Fellowship (BSF) or Community Bible Study (CBS) are near you, these are solid sources for you to access.

How do you know or find out what a church or Christian group believes?

Many have statements of their faith or beliefs on their websites. You can also call and ask about their view of the Bible. If they hedge, keep looking. The first step in the right direction will be the church that has a ready, clear, and concise statement of their belief about the Bible as the inspired Word of God, as opposed to a word of God, or containing the word of God, and so forth.

As of this writing, here are some current teachers you can listen to (and read) for teaching and guidance: Andy Stanley, Ralph Harris, Tim Chalas, Frank Friedmann, Malcolm Smith, Timothy Keller, Tony Evans, and Andrew Farley. If you prefer a female perspective, I suggest Beth Moore, Kay Arthur, Lisa TerKeurst, and Priscilla Shirer.

I also refer you to my writings and books. You can find both at: PrestonGillham.com.

In the "Suggested Resources" of this book, I suggest additional resources to help you ground your faith.

SUGGESTED RESOURCES

PrestonGillham.com

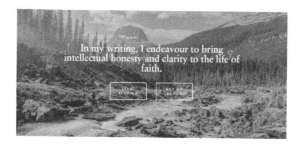

No Mercy— **Preston Gillham**

No Mercy is a sweeping adventure of life, love, trust, and desire - a portrait of the spiritual battle between flesh and spirit, an odyssey asserting that real life is more than meets the eye.

Hank Henderson thought he was going on vacation to Montana, but his brother had something else in mind. Hank's life soon dangles on the precipice of disaster.

Disoriented. Injured. His resources depleted, Hank is caught between powerful forces. One is dark, aggressive, and powerful. The other, of questionable integrity, appears Hank's only option for freedom.

From his placid fishing of Malden Creek into a dungeon of double-dealing. Hank crosses swollen rivers, scales blizzard strewn heights, and discovers more than he bargained for in an unlikely ally.

His hope dependent upon a hesitant trust, Hank gambles to emerge from *No Mercy* a transformed person.

Battle for the Round Tower— **Preston Gillham**

Preston Gillham takes us again into the true world of spiritual life via his novel, *Battle for the Round Tower*.

Returning to Gnarled Wood after two years away, Hank Henderson discovers that the risks have risen. He encounters a dark, spiritual world of subterfuge, black operations, and intrigue.

Powerful beyond what he realizes, Hank wrestles with distrust and doubt to become the man of his destiny.

Through the characters he creates, Preston shows us a powerful people called Believers and Christ-followers.

Confident Woman— **Anabel Gillham**

God does not call women to be perfect. He wants them to be confident—confident in His love and acceptance.

Lifetime Guarantee— **Bill Gillham**

A witty, humorous, and candid book about living as a Christian, what goes wrong, how to remedy your upsets, and your true identity in Christ.

The Reason for God— **Timothy Keller**

Addresses the frequent doubts that skeptics, and even ardent believers, have about religion. Using literature, philosophy, real-life conversations, and potent reasoning, Keller explains how the belief in a Christian God is, in fact, a sound and rational one.

Mere Christianity— **C.S. Lewis**

The most important writer of the 20th century explores the unequaled opportunity for Believers and nonbelievers alike to consider his powerful apologetic for the Christian faith.

More Than a Carpenter— **Josh McDowell**

A brief book of less than 100 pages exploring the Bible, the resurrection, and Christianity.

The Power of the Blood Covenant— **Malcolm Smith**

One message exists to transform the Body of Christ in the twenty-first century: Unraveling the mystery of God's eternal oath.

The Case for Christ— **Lee Strobel**

Strobel cross-examines a dozen experts from schools such as Cambridge, Princeton, and Brandeis, asking hard-hitting questions—and building a captivating case for Christ's divinity.

The Jesus I Never Knew— **Philip Yancey**

Presents a complex character who generates questions as well as answers; a disturbing and exhilarating Jesus who wants to radically transform your life and stretch your faith. Uncovers a Jesus who is brilliant, creative, challenging, fearless, compassionate, unpredictable, and ultimately satisfying.

SUGGESTED WEBSITES

Biblegateway.com

Access and locate resources to study the Bible, search for Scriptures, and explore biblical subjects. Almost every translation of the Bible is readable and searchable.

Lifetime.org

Listen and read about your true identity in Christ and how to live an effective, dynamic life as a Christian.

Network220.org

Locate Christian organizations in your area who teach, train, and guide your walk with Christ and true identity in Him. A good resource for conferences, additional materials, and finding a local church. Organized by States in alphabetical order.

OurResoluteHope.com

This site is the teaching ministry of Pastor Frank Friedmann. Frank is an exegetical Bible teacher—meaning, he teaches the Scripture verse-by-verse, often word-by-word. He is a reliable theologian, intensely practical, honest, transparent, and imminently qualified to speak into your life.

PrestonGillham.com

Read more about Preston, his work, life, and thoughts on life and leadership. This site has an extensive archive of Preston's writing. Subscribe to his blog and stay close to what Preston offers for today's issues from his walk with God. Preston is a therapist and historian by training and a philosopher at heart.

TimothyKeller.com

Tim Keller is a reliable biblical scholar who is a pastor at heart—meaning, he is easy to listen to, practical, and very relevant. He is a brilliant man who readily digests complex concepts and puts them forward for consumption in approachable language. His theology is reformed, which differs from other teachers in this suggested reading list, but that's okay. What Tim teaches is rock-solid reliable. He and his wife, Kathy, also have resources on marriage.

YouVersion.com

This site offers you daily reading plans to help you get started reading the Bible. They also offer discipleship materials, encouraging stories, and a robust app for your device.

ACKNOWLEDGEMENTS

I'm grateful to my advance readers who read *Swagger* before it was ready for prime time. Their feedback, perspective, encouragement, and critique played an invaluable role in preparing *Swagger* for you. Thank you to each.

Lindsay Inman: Thank you for your proofreading, design, layout, and diligent care in giving *Swagger* a compelling appearance.

Abe Martinez: Thank you for editing the audio version of *Swagger*. Because of your diligence and professionalism, the book sounds great.

Lazarus Media Productions: Thank you for helping people know *Swagger* exists. Your marketing expertise, editorial proficiency, and ingenuity are innovative and exemplary. I appreciate and value your partnership.